MORON

THE BEHIND THE SCENES STORY OF MINOR HOCKEY

MORON
The Behind the Scenes Story of Minor Hockey
Copyright © 2013 Todd Millar, *www.toddmillarspeaking.com*

Published by:
Blooming Twig Books
New York / Tulsa
www.bloomingtwig.com

Front cover design by:
Roman Kaufmann
www.desiigo.com

Hardcover: ISBN 978-1-61343-037-8
Paperback: ISBN 978-1-61343-038-5
eBook: ISBN 978-1-61343-039-2

First Edition

For the children of the game.

THE BEHIND THE SCENES STORY OF MINOR HOCKEY

Todd Millar

Blooming Twig Books
New York / Tulsa

TABLE OF CONTENTS

MORON

THE BEHIND THE SCENES STORY OF MINOR HOCKEY

FOREWORD

by JIM PEPLINSKI

What is virtuous about hockey today? What is virtuous about any sport? Why bother playing at all?

When I was a kid 40 years ago, minor and professional sports were more similar than they are today. I believe minor sport today too often imitates the pros, with a misguided view that such imitation is good. Instead, "real" minor sports should continue to focus on teaching our children respect, ethics, honor, teamwork, playing within the rules, the value of relationships, and learning how to win and lose. Professional sport doesn't teach values, it reveals them.

- Real sport is five kids piling into a car, driving to practice, talking about the day, and looking forward to sweating.
- Real sport is a bunch of kids playing road hockey or pick up baseball, and missing dinner because they got so engaged in the game.
- Real sport doesn't require 13-year-olds to wear ties at games, be at the rink 90

minutes before a game, miss school for practices, sit around on expensive ice, straining to hear a coach talking about something, or sitting in the stands counting face offs.

- Real sport is please and thank you.
- Real sport is when your son or daughter loves the sport so much that they will do the dishes and cut the lawn so you get some time to yourself before driving them to their activity.
- Real sport is fast, hard practices with game-like drills that leave you spent after 45 minutes.
- Real sport is hockey, but also swimming, wrestling, badminton, tennis, golf, and soccer – sports that you can play for decades.
- Real sport keeps kids playing, and whether they ever reach a podium or win a Stanley Cup, keeping individuals participating longer is part of the biggest victory – the victory of making a positive difference in someone's life and our community. This is what is virtuous about sport.

There are a number of elements in *Moron: The Behind the Scenes Story of Minor Hockey* that I believe are debatable, including the title. What are not debatable, in my view, are the author's good intentions, accurate observations, and calls to action. Millar has put his integrity and considerable experience into these pages, and it shows. Moron will challenge you to look at the reality of the behaviors and the environment of minor hockey in Canada, and decide if you want to make a difference in the game.

We won't all be lucky enough to play in the NHL or the Olympics, but we can make a very positive difference by ensuring that the real lessons of sport are cemented in our behaviour. When we learn these lessons, we will also perform better in business, and better in life.

Jim Peplinski is a former professional National Hockey League player and captain of the Calgary Flames. He played for the Canadian National Team in the 1988 Winter Olympics, and after ten years in professional hockey, he promised himself that he would retire from hockey if his team won the Stanley Cup. The Flames won in 1989, and Peplinski followed through on his promise. He has since gone on to have many successes in the business sector, including his role as Vice President of Business Development with the only team he competed for, the Calgary Flames.

PREFACE

There is a problem inside of minor hockey. As both a father of a hockey player and as a volunteer at all levels of minor hockey in Canada, I would be hard-pressed to recommend hockey as a place for kids to go and participate in minor sports.

95% of minor hockey is wonderful. The game of hockey is incredible, and I have really enjoyed my time working with my son and countless other kids in the hockey system. But that 5% of problems is a big problem, and could well jeopardize the future of the sport in Canada.[1]

I am only one voice, but I have seen just about every angle of the minor hockey world, from playing hockey as a kid, to being a father on the sidelines during my son's games, to coaching and refereeing countless games, to sitting in boardrooms and talking about the workings of the organization, and finally serving a term as President of Hockey

---

[1] 95% is a subjective and estimated figure. I don't have any concrete studies to support this claim, but would be interested to hear about any, so please drop me a line if you find one. When I refer to this figure throughout the book, it is intended to be an approximation, for the sake of argument.

Calgary (before stepping down amidst controversy surrounding a blog entry I wrote entitled, "Neutrons, Protons, Neurons and Morons," which has since been called, "The Moron Memo").

I share my stories with you between these covers, but my stories are by no means the only stories out there. I would like this to be the beginning of a discussion, because such a conversation is sorely needed, if we are to save our beloved sport of minor hockey in Canada. We need to make change, and it's up to you to join me, and help me to ensure that this sport will remain safe and fun for our children long into the future.

Within minor hockey, I see that we have six main problems. Throughout this book, I attempt to explain why I believe these problems need to be addressed in order to save minor hockey in Canada.

1. Safety of our kids. Especially with regard to body checking.

2. The issue of Fair Play, and the rules and regulations surrounding it.

3. Bullying, which comes in many shapes and sizes inside of the game of hockey.

4. Respect in Sport.

5. Volunteerism, and how we can fix the volunteer system.

6. Adults are the real issue, not the players.

Here's an invitation. Please reach out to me directly via my website, blog, or social media sites (I do monitor them daily), and share your story with me. I know that there are many perspectives on every situation, and I welcome the discussion that will ensue. We all share the common desire to make this sport better, safer, and more fun for our children. So, let's communicate for their sake!

Let's continue the conversation, and always remember, *it's about the kids*.

Todd Millar, March 2013

Hockey Calgary Boss Resigns Over Body Checking "Moron Memo"

September 23, 2012

When contacted late last week regarding a controversial blog of his that used the word moron 14 times to describe those who disagreed with banning hitting in Peewee (ages eleven and twelve), Millar said he'd resign if opposition to his leaked rant grew too loud.

Late Sunday afternoon he made good on that promise, reiterating that he never intended for his blog to be disseminated as it was by minor hockey opponents ...

The blog post was written April 30 in the midst of a campaign aimed at educating parents before a city-wide vote in June that wound up shooting down a body checking ban in Peewee.

- Eric Francis, Calgary Sun

Hockey Calgary President's Resignation Over Critical Blog Post a "Loss" for Organization

September 24, 2012

Hockey Calgary is disappointed their president decided to resign following controversy surrounding a personal blog post in which he decried opponents of banning body checking in Peewee hockey as "morons."

On Sunday, Todd Millar left his volunteer role as president of Alberta's largest minor hockey association after a rant he penned in April and posted on his website was circulated among members of Hockey Calgary ...

Millar told the Herald he was disappointed to leave Hockey Calgary, adding that calling people morons is not how he wanted to end his tenure with the organization.

"There's certainly some disappointment, but I respect the fact that (this) was my own doing," Millar said ...

"Hopefully something good comes from what's transpired here in the last 24 hours," Millar said. "Maybe that's bringing the attention back to the body checking debate."

- Annalise Klingbeil, Calgary Herald

"Neutrons, Protons, Neurons and Morons"
Also known as **"The Moron Memo"**
Published April 30, 2012,[2] on my blog

Neutrons, Protons and Neurons are all common in Science and things I know virtually nothing about. [However] Morons are something that I am becoming all too familiar with in the last few weeks.

Wikipedia defines Morons as [the following]:

> *"Moron" was coined in 1910 from the Ancient Greek word moros, which meant "dull" as opposed to oxy, which meant "sharp", and used to describe a person with a mental age in adulthood of between 8 and twelve. It was once applied to people with an IQ of 51-70, being superior in one degree to "imbecile" (IQ of 26-50) and superior in two degrees to "idiot" (IQ of 0-25). The word moron, along with others including, "idiotic," "imbecilic," "stupid," and "feeble-minded," was formerly considered a valid descriptor in the psychological community, but it is now deprecated in use by psychologists.*

The informal definition or non-clinical definition is one I can relate to given all the current events in my hockey life: "a person who is notably stupid or lacking in good judgment."

I am not a psychologist and I am certainly not about to analyze the term moron or any aspect of the term, however, I most certainly have come to appreciate the relationship between a moron (in

---

[2] Transcript of "Neutrons, Protons, Neurons and Morons," April 30, 2012 (edited for grammar), http://rtmillarholdingsinc.wordpress.com/2012/04 /30/neutrons-protons-neurons-and-morons/. Accessible from the Internet Archive Wayback Machine, http://bit.ly/moron-blog.

the non-clinical sense) and parental behaviour in Hockey. I listened to a young elite hockey player stand before a group of parents [tonight] at a Hockey Calgary [awards banquet]. This young man (17 years of age) made more sense to me then many adults who on a regular basis feel absolutely compelled to expressing their views on every aspect of the key topics in hockey. The young man stood before a room full of adults (100 plus) and shared his view on his experience as a young hockey player growing up in Calgary. At one point he talked about how every year at evaluation time it was the parents who got more excited and bent out of shape than the players. The players just wanted to play hockey. They could care less as to who was on what team or line. It was always the parents who had the issues. A very astute perspective and very accurate from a young man leaving minor hockey.

The game of hockey in the minors, I am told, has always had the issues that it has today. Apparently, we all are supposed to simply accept the game the away it is and never allow any change, even when knowledge is provided that clearly suggests change is required. Yes, I am talking about the body checking debate here in Calgary. Hockey Calgary has made a motion that body checking be removed from Peewee Hockey and parts of Bantam and Midget going forward. Five years of scientific studies and copious amounts of data all point to the rationale. The research, in short, clearly identifies that there is a 33% increase that a player in a body checking Peewee category (ages eleven/twelve) will potentially experience a major injury and/or concussion than a player in a non body checking environment. In other words allow body checking and you will keep the ambulances busy. Don't, and you will save children. How many: 33% of the kids in Calgary playing Peewee (approximately 500 per year). In Calgary, I have been on every radio station, in every paper, many TV stations and on all the major news networks sharing the message. Seems simple, right? Well here is the deal: there are so many morons in this game that cannot understand that by simply changing a simple rule you will save the wellbeing of eleven- and twelve-year-olds. These morons haven't even taken the time to read the research. I would welcome the argument from any one of them if they would simply read the research and provide me any scientific research that argued the data that Hockey Calgary has published on its website. But they cannot. Why? Because it doesn't exist.

So, although it is not politically correct or acceptable in the psychological profession to use the term "moron," Wikipedia does have it right; these parents, hockey fans, and in some cases, custodians of hockey associations (a real embarrassment to volunteerism) truly fit a portion of the definition: a person with a mental age in adulthood between 8 and twelve. I guess I should just ask the kids if they want to have body checking. They just might have a better view on the game than the morons. Just like the young man speaking at the AGM. He gets it.

Apparently this moronic argument is all about development and whether we are developing WHL and NHL hockey players. Well the question so appropriately put to me by one reasonable parent with a recent email asks, "*What level of risk do I feel is acceptable for my child to be exposed to, now knowing the scientific data on the effects on body checking in Peewee hockey?"* Now, that is a sobering question from a non-moron. Yes there are plenty of reasonable people out there; our problem is [that] the morons are louder.

It is said that leadership, and truly leading the way, is a lonely and challenging role. It is, and that statement couldn't be truer. I applaud the Board of Hockey Calgary for all their hard work and their leadership. Their decision and direction is absolutely correct. Children's safety should come before any of the moronic arguments I have heard during the announcement of the motion to change the game.

One can only hope that sanity will prevail. Even the morons say the game is all about fun. I guess [for them] it is fun to watch eleven- and twelve-year-olds getting injured.

Don't give up, Calgary, sanity will prevail and the morons who have opposed so many well-researched things in the past (seat belt laws, smoking age limits, drinking and driving etc.) will lose this battle, too. It is just going to take some time.

Here is to Body Contact, not Body Checking, for the children's sake.

INTRODUCTION
THE MORON MEMO

I wrote my now-infamous "Moron Memo" blog entry (originally called "Neutrons, Protons, Neurons and Morons") on the night of April 30, 2012. Only a few of my closest friends and family saw it – it was on my seldom-visited blog, and I had little notion that the few words of that journal entry would change my life four months later.

I resigned in September 2012 as the President of Hockey Calgary, hoping that my departure would allow the Board of the organization to continue unencumbered in their work to make hockey safer for the children of minor hockey in Calgary. Upon my resignation, I initially felt that all of the work we had done to bring attention to body checking and other dangerous elements of the sport would be lost. Ironically, my resignation from the organization only gave me a bigger platform to work towards change within the system. This book is the continuation of my desire to start a conversation that will reform the sport we all love, and make it safer for our children for generations to come.

It is important to recognize that, although the Moron Memo focused on body checking, this book is about more than simply that one topic. Our beloved game of hockey is faced with great turbulence. It is a well-known fact that the numbers of participation are dropping, immigration patterns are changing, costs are escalating, and the respect element is being called into question on all fronts. This book will cover it all.

I remember growing up playing the game of hockey and hearing the coach tell me, "How are you doing there, Todd?" I was sitting on the bench at the time, after taking a big hit from someone on the other team.

"Well, I'm a little dizzy," I said.

He said with a comforting smile, "Oh, you got your bell rung, did you? You'll be okay."

My coach was a great person, and he didn't know all of the research that we know now. But, in essence, the theory has always been, "Hey, Kid, suck it up!"

Don Cherry famously talked on Canadian television about Russian hockey players supposedly always lying on the ice faking injuries – often implying that "real" hockey players get up, even if they are injured. "Don't be a Russian," is the phrase that many people adopted from Cherry's discussions on the air.

But there's a fundamental difference here. Cherry was talking about professional hockey players who do this for a living. Our kids in minor hockey are just kids. They shouldn't be treated the same way, particularly when their health is in danger.

I have seen countless coaches, parents and others tell our young hockey players, "Get up," "Don't be a Russian," "You just got your bell rung — you'll be fine!" Haven't you? It's a part of our game, and it's something that we have to change.

With all of the information that is now available to us about the dangers of hockey, we know without a shadow of a doubt that our kids are being hurt. What are we going to do about it? It is our responsibility to step up and advocate for our children.

Young children often have their heads down when they are skating. Most of them haven't developed the skills to have their head up all the time. Because of this, when the opposing player (100 pounds) runs into Johnny (70 pounds) at full speed, it's as if he just skated into a brick wall. Johnny lies motionless on the ice, but there's no penalty called.

Guess what? It was a good, fair body check, so there *was* no penalty.

You can hear a pin drop in the arena as little Johnny lies motionless on the ice. Obviously, he is concussed. He is in disarray. We have allowed the game to have body checking in it. Little Johnny is now lying on the ice.

The coach and the referee come over, and they call 911. They don't touch little Johnny because they don't know what's wrong with him. Is he concussed? Did he break his neck? Did he break his back? What has happened?

When it's your child lying motionless on the ice, your heart stops, and terror creeps in. What has happened to your eleven-year-old boy? I have seen this happen many times, and every time, a mom or dad will take in a breath, run to the rink-side, anxiously hoping their child will be okay. If this has happened to you, you know the sinking, terrified feeling that takes over your entire being. You are responsible for their welfare, and you feel helpless.

At some point, I didn't really believe that body checking was a serious issue. But once I saw the data, and I watched injuries happen on the ice, I realized that something had to be done. What I don't understand is, if parents, coaches, and others have seen the same data that I have, why don't they support a safer environment for their young children?

I'm not saying that injuries should never happen. All sports carry risks. If you are on the monkey bars and fall off, you could break your arm. If you are playing baseball and a ball hits you in the head, you could get a concussion. If you play football, you could dislocate a shoulder. There are many dangerous things that can happen as a result of sports. Hockey is no different. If you put a kid out there with skates, heavy equipment, a hard surface, and then tell them to skate as fast as they can, and hit a hard black piece of rubber as hard as they can, there will be injuries.

The point is not that there won't be any injuries at all, but that we can reduce the number of serious injuries in our children if we only change one element of the game. Kids have plenty to learn at that age about every other aspect of the game. Why not make their lives safer?

Research has shown that regulating body checking won't affect kids' ability to become future NHL stars. In fact, several NHL players have gone on record supporting this very research.

Here are the statistics: 33 percent more young hockey players in Calgary are hurt than respective children in Quebec (where body checking has been outlawed for 25 years in the Peewee age group). Extrapolated outwards, if kids play hockey in a body checking league, they are much more likely to have a serious injury (missing two or more games because of injury) than a non-body checking league. Yet we still allow our kids to get out on the ice, despite the dangers. We know that hundreds more of them will be significantly injured because of our complacency, yet we do nothing. It's time to change that.

We would never allow our kids to go to Playground A if we knew that Playground B was safer. If your kids were to go to Playground A, they would be 33 percent more likely to be seriously hurt. Would you send your kids to play there?

Safety is a critical issue in minor hockey, and it is the issue that eventually led to my resignation as President of Hockey Calgary (as I mentioned previously, as a result of the body checking debate and my "Moron Memo"). However, it is not the intention of this book to singularly focus on this topic. There is one issue, however, that permeates my entire narrative: the problem in minor hockey is not the kids – it's the adults.

If you send your little boy to play at Playground A, I think I can safely call you a moron.

Following a successful career in business (see my book Boardroom to Base Camp), I decided to spend a great deal more time with my children and family. Because my son, at the time, was in minor hockey, I volunteered with his team, and then as a member of the Hockey Calgary Board of Directors, finally being appointed the President of Hockey Calgary in June 2011.

At that same meeting, the Hockey Calgary Board agreed to form a committee that would review all of the body checking data available, and come back on a recommendation for how the association could make the environment safer for participants. This was done as a response to a direct request from the members at the AGM when I was voted in as President. Therefore, I also saw my charge as the new President of Hockey Calgary to work hard on the topic of body checking – since this was clearly one of the key mandates given to the Board at that time.

Within the following months, we worked to assemble a Body Checking Review Committee made up of twelve members across minor hockey in Calgary, of various demographic profiles. Members of the committee came together on a regular basis, and began to review the data in front of them. The committee's goal was to give recommendations back to the Board – they wouldn't be making the decisions themselves. I met with them on several occasions, and made sure there was clarity around their important role in this debate. All of the data showed that, if we wanted the game to be safer, we should take the body checking element out. Having said this, the committee was to be impartial and review all of the data, and come back with the direction that was supporting the membership's request. That in itself became a problem with some of the committee members who clearly arrived at the table with subjective viewpoints.

While there was a general consensus among the many, there were a few very vocal individuals who didn't like the message. They didn't like the change that was going on. At this point, we still had hope that we could make the change our kids needed. Unfortunately, these people were eventually able to slow the progress towards needed reform in Hockey Calgary.

The discussion continued through the rest of 2011, and into the first part of 2012, and the Body Checking Review Committee continued to review data and was close to making a recommendation. Near the close of the season, in late February 2012, the committee notified me that the committee had come up with a 52-page report.

The Board analyzed and reviewed the report on body checking on two separate occasions. I was also present at those meetings, but was not allowed to vote (unless there was a tie). A total of ten hours of meeting time was dedicated to that one topic, and at the end, a majority of the Directors voted to remove body checking in Peewee and a second motion would be prepared for the consideration of the removal of body checking in the lower categories of Bantam and Midget.

These motions, and the direction which Hockey Calgary intended to take minor hockey are announced through what I still today believe to be an extremely effective communication process. First, we announced it to the 24 community presidents in Calgary via conference call, and the next day, we had a press conference that was well attended by media outlets in town.

Anyone who has had training in the area of media relations, or has ever been charged with the release of critical and sensitive information, would agree with the discreet process that Hockey

Calgary employed for this rollout. It was professional, and paid particular attention to avoiding leaks. It was a well-orchestrated plan by Hockey Calgary.

This is when the real "fun" began. I hit the road and talked with as many hockey communities as I could, educating the members on the decision the Board had made, and the recommendation that would be tabled at the June AGM. There were an overwhelming number of supporters of these new changes, but there was a very vocal minority that didn't like the changes we were proposing, and would block them in whatever way they could.

At these various functions I began to learn the complacency that exists among strong supporters of the issue. It became clear to me that people understood the importance of the issue, but in many cases didn't feel the need to express their point of view at meetings. Of course it made sense to take body checking out of the category of Peewee. All the data was clear. But the complacent majority failed to accurately gauge the aggressiveness of the detractors.

At every meeting, I was accused of "killing the game," removing the chances of children in Calgary to make the NHL. My favourite line was someone who said I was the "champion of the *pussification* of hockey." I was approached by hostile moms and dads, guys wearing "hit hard" t-shirts, and people with arms crossed over their chests who stared me down as if I was their direct enemy. Nevertheless, I continued to give invited informational sessions across the city.

Finally, we come to the night of my "Moron" blog post. On the evening of April 30, 2012 (seven weeks prior to the scheduled Hockey Calgary vote on body checking), I attended the Annual Awards Recognition Banquet for Hockey Calgary. It was a difficult time for me, as my father was in the hospital, but I was looking forward to making the most of an evening that celebrated the key players in our organization. And I was happy that I wouldn't have to speak about body checking that night. Instead, I was given the honor of addressing the attendees, and I spoke from the heart. I expressed my affection for the sport, and how our organization made the great city of Calgary an even better place.

Later in the evening, we had two young hockey players go up onto the platform and speak about their experiences in minor hockey. They spoke very passionately about the game, and had a message for all of us. They didn't care about all of the evaluations, what team they played on, and all the rest. They just loved the game. I was proud when they mentioned Hockey Calgary's efforts at the time to champion the "Respect in Sport" initiative that had so much success – it was incredible to hear such optimism and encouragement from the mouths of our youth leaders. They truly believed in the simplicity of the game. They just wanted to go out and play hockey, and love the game.

At that moment, it was as if a pebble dropped into a pool of clear water. All of the crap I had been going through behind the scenes seemed ridiculous. The parents, coaches, Board Members, and I were all there to be custodians of the game, so that it would stay simple and beautiful for these kids. It was our responsibility to keep the game safe and fun. It was, and still is, so clear to me what was important to those teenaged boys.

The rest of that night, various people came up to me and reinforced their very vocal desire for us to lay off the body checking issue. They didn't want this change, and they would do whatever was in their power to make sure it didn't happen. I received their criticisms with a smile, and did my best to internalize all of their arguments. We had hashed all of this out before, and it was certainly not going to be the last time I took criticism.

I arrived home around ten p.m. that night, conflicted. On one hand, I carried with me the incredible optimism and enthusiasm I had seen in the young men's speeches. On the other hand, the arguments of a vocal (and angry) minority rang inside of my head as well. I needed to process what I had heard, and what I believed, so I did what I often do. I wrote a journal entry for my friends and family, and posted it to my blog. I received a comment or two about it, but then I didn't think about it again until five months later.

After I wrote my blog entry, several months passed. The body checking vote at the AGM came and went, and the motion to remove body checking was defeated. But there was still plenty of work to be done and the board was working hard on our strategic plan and direction. We focused not only on the body checking initiative, but on anti-bullying, and all kinds of reforms that would improve Hockey Calgary over the long-term. Let's just say that I didn't make friends in certain communities during that time; people who had been abusing the system and bullying players and parents were now being confronted, and it was not easy for them to make the changes we were asking them to make. These coaches and others acted as if they were not accountable to anyone; almost as if they were independent elites who were starting their own farm system for the NHL. We saw what this was doing to the kids, and we did our best to intervene.

Because of my work with the Board, and the countless hours of the time we spent trying to reform Hockey Calgary for the better, a group of individuals rose up against me. In their opinion, I was making too many changes, too quickly (even though most of the members of Hockey Calgary embraced those changes). One individual in particular ("I'll call him "Mr. P.") had it out for me, and made it his mission to take me down. He also happened to be a newly-elected member of the Hockey Calgary Board, and was one of the "old guard" who was set in his ways, but rarely provided any credible direction to the debates of the day.

In August 2012, Mr. P. got his chance when he was presumably trolling the Internet for dirt on me, and came across my personal blog. Even though only a handful of people had ever seen the entry I wrote about "Morons" on my blog, Mr. P. had found his pot of gold. He would publicize the entry in order to discredit the work I had been doing with Hockey Calgary.

First, Mr. P. brought a printout of this blog article to the attention of the elite council, and shared it with all of the leaders there. I also had a couple of Board Members at that meeting, and they reported this back to me that there had been heated discussions about this blog article. Apparently, they spoke about how they could "take me down."

"Take me down?"

This was an interesting comment that resonated with me very much. I was a volunteer president who gave 30 hours a week to my duties, and they wanted to *take me down*. This was the opportunity they had been looking for to get me out of the system – they were hoping that I would then stop causing them problems.

Mr. P.'s next step was to contact Eric Francis, the sports columnist of a local newspaper, who covered a good number of hockey stories, and told him that he had a great scoop – one that would cause all kinds of controversy.

Francis held onto the blog entry for a few days, considering what to write. Then he called me. I vividly remember the conversation. He said, "Hey, Todd, how are you doing?"

I knew Francis from other media appearances I had done. He continued, "I wanted to talk to you, and get your opinion on the lockout that's going on in the NHL."

I knew immediately that Francis was up to something. At the time, the NHL lockout was in full swing, but he certainly wouldn't be calling me to ask about that. I said to him, pointedly, "Are you kidding me, Eric? Really?" It was obvious to me that he had called about something else. I asked, skeptically, "Are you really calling me up to talk about a lockout in the NHL?"

He then told me about the blog entry, and we had a frank and open discussion about it. I told him the truth, and I also told him that he had a choice whether to publish the article or not. He chose to publish, and I did what I had to do – I resigned my presidency, so that the Board wouldn't have to deal with the fallout from this controversy.

Ironically, my foes thought that I would be out of the picture if they brought this "Moron" blog entry to light. Instead, it has brought even more attention to the issue of body checking than ever before, and has forged inside of minor hockey the energy and willpower to draw even more attention to its major problems. I now have been given a wonderful platform to talk about these issues, and am no longer encumbered by the mantle of President, and can speak freely about what I have seen in minor hockey over my years there.

I have now done numerous interviews as the former president of Hockey Calgary, and been called upon as an expert on body checking and other dangers in minor hockey. We received cards and letters from all across Canada, talking about why we need to ban body checking, and what we can do to change things. Thanks to Eric Francis, Mr. P., the elite council, and my other detractors, the topic is front and center once again.

As a result of my resignation, I am now able to go and do more things, and I don't have to be sensitive to my former role as President of Hockey Calgary. I am just a Canadian citizen who has all the facts and data about this subject, and now I am able to express my opinion freely.

Hockey is a great game. It is a passionate game. It has been said that it is a religion in Canada, and perhaps there's some truth in that. We watch the arenas fill up every single night, and every weekend, and we watch our kids go in, and for the most part, have an unbelievable experience. That is the way it should be. Throughout this book, you will hear me say over and over again, the problem is the adults and not the kids. Let's take a pledge to make sure we keep our kids as safe as possible. Game on!

MORON
THE BEHIND THE SCENES STORY OF MINOR HOCKEY

PART ONE:
THE GAME

Chapter One
WHAT RESPECT ?

S uddenly, as I looked down the ice, I saw at the other corner of the rink a father banging on the glass, yelling at the young officials on the ice, screaming at the top of his lungs, "Are you blind? How could you make that call? You idiot!" He was pointing his finger aggressively at the teenaged officials on the ice.

My volunteer position at the time in Hockey Calgary was "league chair" – and part of my duty was to watch the behaviours of people and make sure that the respect component of the game was being upheld.

A league chair in the hierarchy of Hockey Calgary was basically responsible for looking after a particular age category, and in my case it was two divisions in the Peewee category. So, we are talking about eleven- and twelve-year-olds. My role as a league chair was to go out and watch hockey games, talk to the coaches, and make sure that they were following the proper policies inside of the game. At the end of the game you would report the scores and do some administrative tasks to make sure that the function of hockey was, in my particular category, being fulfilled.

I started to walk towards the shouting man from 200 feet away. Moms and dads and sisters and brothers and grandparents were all in the stands that day as was typically the fashion, sitting on blankets or little seat cushions. They all turned their heads in the direction of this man.

As I began to walk more quickly, I could see that this father was violently angry. His face was bright red as he screamed, and the veins on his neck were popping. At this point, he put his leg up on the boards – he was a tall man – and he reached up, clinging to the glass. As a superhero (or super-villain) might have done, this irate father had Spi-der-Manned himself up the side of the glass at the side of the hockey rink, and was now peering over the top edge of the glass, yelling at the top of his lungs at the teenaged officials. He was screaming every name you could possibly imagine at these poor young referees on the ice.

I arrived at the scene, and tugged on the man's pant leg, asking him to step down off of the glass. He abruptly turned to me, and asked me, "Who the hell are you?"

I replied, as calmly as I could muster, "I'm with Hockey Calgary. I'd like you to step down, and then we can talk."

I was astounded at this man's behaviour, and it didn't seem possible that this grown man had climbed up the 15-foot tall wall of the ice rink to scream at the referees from what he saw as a better vantage point.

After a bit more screaming, he finally realized I was serious, and that I wanted him to step down.

After jumping down, I pulled him aside and I asked him, "Do you have a son out there?"

His voice laced with anger, he defensively offered, "Yes, I do."

I told him, very simply, "I can't imagine that your young son, eleven years old, is very proud of his dad at this moment."

My calm, yet stern words seemed to resonate with him, and he seemed to calm down. We had a reasonable discussion about his behaviour, but at the end of that conversation, I asked him to leave the hockey rink.

After the game that night, I remember thinking to myself, *What's going on here?* We are talking about a *game* that has eleven- and twelve-year-olds out there skating on the ice.

Unfortunately, this was not the only time I had to escort someone from a hockey rink. But it was one of the most memorable. I'll never forget Spider-

Man. But it really makes you wonder what takes over someone like that. His behaviour was moronic, and he was behaving at the level of intelligence of a child, without any rationale, and without any respect at all.

What happens to these people? They temporarily take off the hat of their everyday life and they put on a *Moron Helmet*. For whatever reason, near that hockey rink, they think that aggressive, asinine behaviour is acceptable, for those few moments of watching their son or daughter play the game of hockey. Would they act like that in front of their boss, or at a family function? I hope not. But they do act that way at a hockey rink.

There is an incredible YouTube video by Miller Donnelly, who was nine years old when he first recorded it in 2008 (http://bit.ly/magic-helmet). He speaks about his *Magic Helmet* in that video. When he puts it on, suddenly everyone treats him like an adult, and he's no longer a nine-year-old boy. Everyone is yelling and screaming at the top of their lungs at him.

As I mentioned above, in the same way the young hockey player feels like he puts on a *Magic Helmet*, his parents, coaches, and others put on a *Moron Helmet*, and do crazy things like scream at young boys playing a game on the ice. Or climb the glass of a hockey rink like Spider-Man.

Let me be perfectly honest here. I've had my *Moron Helmet* moments too. I understand it. We all have our moments in time where we experience some degree of behaviour that we, in hindsight, look back on and think, *Boy, that wasn't very respectful!*

I get it. We all have those moments in life. The problem is that, in the game of minor hockey in Canada, *Moron Helmets* are far too common.

Contrary to some people's belief, it is possible to change moronic behaviour, and it's something we need to work harder on. I remember being at a meeting with some of the "old guard" in hockey at a Hockey Canada AGM, when one particular leader within the organization made a comment that it's always been this way, and it will always be this way in the future. I don't ascribe to that point of view. I believe that kind of thinking is just as moronic as Spider-Man's behaviour on that glass.

It's not just angry fathers that cause trouble in minor hockey. There are coaches, mothers, grandparents, and the kids themselves, sometimes causing problems, fights, and so forth. Hockey Calgary has rules to take care of difficult situations, as do minor hockey associations across Canada. As we will discuss later, it is not about the rules, but rather the disciplined application of the rules. In any case, there is something fundamentally odd about the *Moron Helmet*. People simply act differently around the sport of hockey, even when it is played by small children.

Another example I remember quite vividly of moronic behaviour was when two mothers from opposing teams got into a fistfight. Long story short, the two moms ended up in fist-a-cuffs, screaming at one another all the way out of the building.

I also remember a father who decided to stand up at the top of the bleachers and yell profanities at the top of his lungs – directed at the rookie twelve-year-old official who was on the ice. His behaviour was so disturbing, that the game had to be stopped, and would not continue until he was removed from the premises, escorted out by fellow parents in order for the game to proceed.

One very upsetting case involved a league chair, who asked a parent to calm down, and was physically threatened. The league chair resigned on the spot, and was escorted through the Zamboni ice entrance by other parents to safety. The hockey rink attendant that day had to call the police in order to remove the angry parent.

The list goes on and on of the inappropriate behaviour from people behind the glass, not to mention the issue that happens on the rink with coaches' behaviour towards on-ice officials. Unfortunately, I have seen file after file of disrespectful behaviour from all types of volunteers at every level in the minor hockey system.

I recall one situation where a young official would not even go into the dressing room after a hockey game because the coach had completely chastised and been disrespectful to him, a 14-year-old boy.

The coach had not stoped yelling at him at the top of his lungs, even when the team was shaking hands at the end of the hockey game. The coach continued to berate the official, telling him he had done a terrible job. By the end of it, the boy was in tears, and refused to go into the referee's dressing room that night. The next day, the boy's parents called Hockey Calgary and told us that their son had not even attended school the following day.

Anyone that hears these stories, or has witnessed these stories would absolutely agree that such behaviour is moronic and has to change. It all starts with the majority; most of the people in that hockey arena do not behave this way, and if they start taking action against those who behave that way, we will be able to fix the problem.

One initiative that has had a great deal of success is the Respect in Sport program.[3] Hockey Calgary, Hockey Alberta, and then Hockey Canada have made this a part of their outreach into the community. Unfortunately, this is not a mandatory program for all parents, and I seriously doubt that parents like Spider-Man will log in to the online training anytime soon. But it's a start, and a great one.

We need to have a bottom-up approach. The rules and punishments are there, and they have been

---

[3] Respect Group (www.respectgroupinc.com) was started in 2004, and has as its mission to "recognize and prevent abuse, bullying, and harassment through interactive, online certification." They work in collaboration with the Canadian Red Cross, and their e-learning platform has the goal of "inspiring a global culture of respect."

spelled out for many, many years in the different rulebooks that are available, whether it be the Hockey Canada rulebook or the particular branch rulebook or the direct association rulebook. In most cases those rules are well laid out and communicated throughout the organizations. The problem is the ability to enforce the rules and embrace the rules.

Here is the way we need to go about making change. There are three critical components to the success of this game:

1. On-ice officials who govern the on-ice behaviour of the game, under the complete direction of the rulebook that is authored by Hockey Canada.

2. Coaches who have to be recruited by various hockey associations, are properly certified, and are abiding by all the rules.

3. Adults: parents and volunteers.

You can't rely on any of these three groups independent of the other groups. But when all three are well-regulated and respectful, the three-legged stool will stand firm. We all know what happens to a stool if it is missing a leg – it's falling over. Unfortunately, when I talk about the moronic behaviour that's happening inside the game of hockey, it's inevitably because one of those three legs is damaged, or has fallen off altogether.

The majority of on-ice officials, coaches, parents and volunteers are great people. I am not suggesting that they are all *Morons*, by any means. There are a few *Morons* in each category, but society has great success at resolving problems when "great" people get involved and address moronic behaviour. There are vehicles and processes to follow to deal with the *Morons*.

Too many great people in this game in all three categories don't step up to the plate and call out the problems. Often, parents won't speak up out of fear, or because they feel that they don't want to get involved because "this too will pass." I hear these kind of stories *all* the time. They all end with a sad statement such as, "If I do that my kid won't be on that team next year." Who is being bullied in this situation?

All three parties should embrace the fact that they have an obligation to understand the rules, understand the consequences and keep things in perspective. What it comes down to is that this is a game for children, of whom 99% are not going into professional sports. These kids are only on the rink for the full purpose of camaraderie, learning how to work together, engaging in some exercise, and darn it, just having some fun.

The Respect in Sport initiative is a great place to begin. It is a great tool for parents to understand the behaviours that are acceptable, respectful, and disrespectful. It really focuses parents on policing themselves, but also gives parents skills and empowerment so that, when they see something that's inappropriate, they will know what actions to take. When parents see Spider-Man climbing the glass, or two moms duking it out in the stands, other parents need to step up – they can't just sit back and be oblivious.

If you see disrespectful or inappropriate behaviour, you have to step up, and you have to communicate with your local minor hockey association, which can give you tools for these situations. Do not allow yourself to be bullied, and if you don't get immediate help, keep going up the ladder until you get answers.

Also, we need to empower parents to communicate with coaches in the same way they should communicate with other parents. If coaches aren't keeping things in perspective, they might need a little tug on their pants just like Spider-Man did. Look at that coach, and realize that he has a *Moron Helmet* on. Remind him that this isn't what we are all here for – it's about the kids, and the love of sport. Tell him that he is not modeling the behaviour he should be in front of impressionable children.

Let's not forget Spider-Man. I know I won't. Imagine the number of people who were affected by his behaviour that day. There were 19 kids on each team – that makes 38 total. The stands had more than 200 people in them. That's 238 people total. And two twelve-year-old officials on the ice, who were being yelled at for a missed offside call. All of this during an eleven- and twelve-year-old Peewee hockey game.

I would hazard to guess that, if I could find Spider-Man today, I'm quite sure that he would look back and say, "You know what? I really did have *Moron Helmet* on that day. I really did behave like a moron."

Spider-Man probably would be a little embarrassed, and might even have changed his behaviour since then. But the damage that is done by that type of behaviour inside of a rink filled with so many impressionable kids is irreparable. Such reckless disregard for Respect in Sport has to be stopped. I challenge you to help me get started.

Chapter Two
BODY CHECKING

June 2011. Welcome to the role as President of Hockey Calgary. First motion of business: proposed wording of the following motion.

> The Hockey Calgary Executive Committee is instructed by the membership to establish a sub-committee at the start of the 2011 / 2012 hockey season for the purposes of reviewing the impact of body checking in all levels of hockey where body checking is currently allowed. The sub-committee is to report back to the Board of Directors with recommendations on how to enhance player safer with a focus on injury reduction associated with potential continued inclusion or removal of body checking in Peewee hockey.

Rationale for changing the motion:

> The sub-committee is expected to review current research and studies that are available on the topic in order to finalize once and for all an association wide position on the sensitive issue of body checking in minor hockey.

The previous motion is the actual request from the members at large going into my year as President. Little did I know what lay ahead. At the time, this motion seemed to be a crystal clear mandate. Indeed, if we are actually desiring the way forward to enhance player safety, then the answer is crystal clear. Unfortunately, our "mandate" was built on a foundation of sand.

There is no way that you will send your son to a school that is 33% more dangerous than your other choice. You won't introduce him to a babysitter who is 33% more likely to hurt him. And you won't give him food that is 33% more likely to cause cancer. So, why would you want your son to engage in body checking in Peewee hockey, when you know that he is 33% more likely to get hurt?

I recently heard the argument that people die in cars, and that hasn't stopped us from driving. Sorry, but that is the type of moronic comment we are up against. You would be shocked if you knew who said it.

We are talking about major injuries here, defined as injuries that mean lost time from the game of hockey, including broken limbs, concussions, and many other terrible possibilities. We will talk about concussions more in Chapter Three, but they are a big consequence of body checking in the minor leagues.

When it comes down to it, we know our kids will get hurt far less often if we simply cease to allow them to body check until they are older. We will reduce the number of concussions, and all physical injuries. Why do we want them to continue body checking one another in the face of all of the evidence? It's moronic.

It was easy for us to commission a study that researched the effects of body checking. But do we have the strength to act on those results? After countless hours of research, review, and a seven-year timetable, two scientists came back with incredibly significant results. We decided that their findings were significant enough to create a committee that would investigate the matter.

An important point to reference here is the members were already surveyed by an independent firm, Provoke. 3600 people participated in the survey and Hockey Calgary broke the data down by community. All of the information was made readily available to all and continues to be available on www.hockeycalgary.ca, the Hockey Calgary website. A majority, more than 50 percent of those surveyed, wanted a safer environment from body checking for children in Peewee.

The committee's 52-page document basically told the Hockey Calgary Board, *Remove body checking.* Here's where things get strange. What happens as a result? Was the proposal accepted by the heads of the hockey associations that were a part of Hockey Calgary? No. Eight of the 24 hockey associations in our organization decided that they didn't like that message. They wanted to keep body checking, despite the risks.

Believe it or not, those presidents and leaders decided not to engage families in their associations, and instead, decided to derail the entire debate, and bully some of the other presidents into joining them.

What was their argument against body checking? They had three main points:

1. Kids wouldn't be allowed to play in tournaments, because other associations had body checking.
2. The young players' hockey development would be negatively impacted.
3. Let others implement these changes first.

My answers to those three points are as follows:

1. Kids would be able to play in tournaments without any trouble; the reality is that tournament play amounts to three or four games of a 20-game season, and there are plenty of areas to go to play in tournaments that likewise would not allow body checking.
2. NHL players have come out to talk about this, and studies also show the opposite of what our detractors believed. Young players might even show better development when body checking is not in the equation during development years. Additionally, USA Hockey had just completed a study clearly identifying that children in this age

category do not have the cognitive learning ability to successfully include body checking in their game play.

3. The data show that our children will be safer with a few common sense regulations. There's no reason to wait.

Long story short, when all of the presidents and leaders in Hockey Calgary came together, they took a vote that was not indicative of the general public's desire to eliminate body checking. They overturned the decision that the Board of Hockey Calgary had made. Body checking would stay, at least for now.

Let's talk about body checking for a moment. Injuries don't just happen when body checking is done illegally. A legal hit can cause serious damage to kids this age. We're not talking about some wingnut's behaviour, throwing a stick around or hitting a guy in the head. We are talking about an open ice body check that results in a child being injured.

The purpose of a body check is to gain possession of the puck. Essentially, this means that you are moving the opponent off the puck for the sole purpose of gaining possession of the puck. It's not as simple as it sounds. When two hockey players hit one another this way, they will do a few different (legal) things. They might rub you, push you up against the boards, or body check you on the open ice. And as long as your hands are down, and you're not making any kind of upper body gesture to the person's head or sticking your knee out, body checking is allowed.

For further reference here is the clearly articulated excerpt from Hockey Canada:

The Hockey Canada Four-Step Checking Model

- *Step #1 – Positioning and Angling*
  The first step in teaching Checking is to learn how to control skating and establish position to approach the opponent from an angle minimizing time and space for the opponent.

- *Step #2 – Stick Checks*
  The second step is to effectively use the stick, poke checking and sweep checking, lifting and locking the opponent's stick.

- *Step #3 – Body Contact*
  The third step is to use the body to block the opponent's way or take away the skating lanes of another player. The correct stance and effective use of leg strength are important parts of these techniques.

- *Step #4 – Body Checking*
  The fourth and final step is actual body checking. This step includes teaching techniques to check and receive a body check as well as safety and rules.

Unfortunately, body checking has taken on a life of its own, and sometimes isn't used only to take control of the puck. In other words, Hockey Canada's Four-Step Checking Model isn't being followed. It's become at times an aggressive act. If one player has his head down, skating with the puck, the defender is allowed to literally ram right into him on the open ice, throwing him off the puck. This can cause serious damage to the player being hit, especially if they didn't see the hit coming. Although, according to the rules, that's a legal hit because you did not hit the player's head, you did not stick your knee out, and you did it with your body and your arms forward across your chest, you might have seriously injured the other player, especially if they are smaller than you are. In the eleven- to twelve-year-old Peewee category in particular, these children are still trying to learn how to handle the stick, pass the puck, and skate, not protect themselves from body checks on the open ice.

At the end of the day, they are just kids. We are talking about Fourth and Fifth Graders – that time in life where everyone varies dramatically in shape and size. One little guy is scrawny and barely tall enough to go on amusement park rides, and another one looks like he's already in full-blown puberty.

Furthermore, these kids are just learning how to body check, and are highly reliant on their coach to teach them about this strange and frightening new aspect of the game. We rely on volunteers to teach kids about body checking, and hope that they receive consistent training, but we can't be sure. So, we have Fourth and Fifth Graders on the ice, most of them have never had body checking ever in their life, and most of them have not had the full-fledged coaching experience they would need to teach them how to give and receive proper body checks. This situation is an accident waiting to happen.

I recall one situation quite vividly, involving a rather large boy and a relatively small boy, both of them in their first year of the Peewee category, during the third game of the season. The smaller eleven-year-old was skating out of his defensive zone during the game, and clearly had his head down. As he crossed the blue line, the larger boy did a textbook job of body checking the small boy, and stood the kid right up as he skated towards him. This was a legal body check. The large boy's arms were down, and he didn't hit the smaller boy's head. He simply made a good, solid body check.

Of course, what happened to that small child is that he was thrust down on the ice in a very, very impactful way. He lay there motionless. The air left the room as the stands became silent.

An NHL player never would have put himself in that position. First off, he would have had his head up, and he would have been looking around. And second of all, the opposing player wouldn't have been given the opportunity to give that kind of body check.

The problem here is that you have a system, in particular in the Peewee age category, where you have young or less seasoned coaches, and young players who are inexperienced with the concept of body checking. There are ways of educating the giving and receiving of body checks, but coaches aren't doing it correctly all the time, so there are big risks to these kids as a result.

In Hockey Calgary, we were responsible for 1,500 Peewee children, who mostly had coaches with very little experience. Layer that on top of Moms and Dads (particularly Dads) who were probably raised in an environment of "Suck it up," and "You just got your bell rung."

Little Johnny was lying motionless on the ice, and several of the parents had now come closer to the glass, to see if Johnny was going to be okay. Presumably one of those parents was Johnny's mother, gasping and horrified at the thought that her son was lying there motionless on the ice, facedown.

At the same time, from the other side of the rink, Coach Smith is scooting across the ice in his tennis shoes towards little Johnny. The referees were standing 20-30 feet away, talking to one another.

These teenaged boys would have been scared that they had missed a call that might have led to this moment.

The coach, of course, while shuffling across the ice, is letting a few choice words fly out of his mouth in the direction of the referees who, in his opinion, have missed a call. Unfortunately, the fact that little Johnny is lying on the ice doesn't mean he was fouled. In this case, he had been legally checked, even though he seemed to be very hurt by the hit.

When the coach reached little Johnny, it becomes pretty clear that Johnny is terrified, scared more than anything over the fact that he's just had this huge, huge hit; he still lay motionless on the ice. Thankfully the coach didn't try to move him initially, and he allowed Johnny to decide of his own accord whether he could move or not.

For a few minutes, all of the parents pressed up against the glass, watching, the referees stood a good distance away, and the players were all assigned back to their benches. You could hear a pin drop in the arena, as this ten-year-old Fourth Grader was lying on the ice motionless. Thankfully, eventually Johnny was able to, of his own accord, roll over and sit up. He was visibly shaken up by this, and was in tears. He was helped to his feet, and thankfully, he was not severely injured.

This situation, in particular, ended well. Johnny returned to the bench, and a few shifts later, he was back skating. However, all too often, the outcome of such an accident is a little bit different.

Within this book so far, I've spoken out mostly about body checking among eleven- to twelve-year-old children in the Peewee age group. But I personally believe that there shouldn't be body checking in any children's leagues, except for possibly the most elite groups. Hockey for 99% of these children is about camaraderie and enjoyment – not unlike within adult recreational, or "beer" leagues.

What is interesting is that, within beer league or recreational hockey for adults, there is no body checking. Why? Because the businesspeople who play in those leagues need to wake up the next day to go to work. Shouldn't we be thinking the same thing about our children? If they get hit too hard, they may not be able to go to school. Isn't there something the matter with this?

On a snowy day in Calgary, I look out my window and see kids playing on the pond that's just over the hill. That's what hockey is all about. It's about kids having fun. That's where this game came from. And it's what we need to remember at the ice arena.

This nostalgic memory of playing on a pond outside in the middle of the winter conflicts directly with the vision of some parents and coaches in our current environment. They want their team to win at all costs, and they want their kid to end up in the NHL and get fame and fortune. Believe it or not, this is one of the main arguments against the elimination of body checking at the Peewee level.

Some coaches and parents believe that their kids need to start learning to body check at age eleven, or they won't be able to get into the NHL. We tested that hypothesis, and we spoke to several members of the NHL, and to other experts as well.

Hockey Calgary board had an NHL advisory board that was put together by alumni from the NHL. The general manager and I met with those individuals and asked them to be part of our advisory board. They attended a couple of meetings with us and on that agenda was the topic of body checking.

Every single NHL player on that advisory board said, given the data available and their personal experience, that it made no sense to keep body checking in Peewee. Not one of them argued the point of leaving it in.

After reading all of my impassioned rhetoric about the perils of body checking, you will be surprised to hear that I was the guy on the Hockey Calgary Board who didn't want to get rid of body checking when I first saw the result of Dr. Carolyn Emery's study.[4] I was the person sitting in that room saying, "You have got to be kidding me. You shouldn't take body checking out of Peewee – you're going to hurt the kids in the next level up, Bantam. We have to leave it in!"

---

[4] Study also includes Dr. Carolyn Emery's colleagues: Jian Kang, PhD, Ian Shrier, MD, PhD, Claude Goulet, PhD, Brent E. Hagel, PhD, Brian W. Benson, MD, PhD, Alberto Nettel-Aguirre, PhD, Jenelle R. McAllister, MSc, Gavin M. Hamilton, MSc, Willem H. Meeuwisse, MD, PhD.

Body Checking Fast Facts

- Body Checking is the single most consistent risk factor for injury to minor hockey players.
- Body Checking is associated with between 45 and 86 percent of injuries in minor hockey.
- Kids who body check at the Peewee level are three times more likely to suffer from a concussion or major injury.
- Deferring body checking to Bantam will allow for further focus on skill development at the Peewee level rather than players skating around trying to deliver body checks, or avoid body checks.
- The introduction of body checking at any age will increase injuries.
- The evidence speaks to concussions occurring in higher levels of pee wee, (divisions 1-3) not lower ones. Making the decision to keep it in higher levels would be contraindicated by the evidence.
- Concussions are especially damaging to younger children and could have a longer term affect on their health than those who might become concussed later in life.

- Skill level development actually goes up when body checking is removed. Hockey USA has revealed their own study that showed kids learn and practice better fundamental skills when hitting is removed from the category. There is less intimidation in the game and more room to work on hockey skills.
- Peewee players who wish to play at the elite level will not be affected, they will still be taught the fundamentals of body checking in practices which will prepare them for the future.
- According to Dr. Caroyln Emery's findings, Peewee Players make up 60 percent of concussion cases in Hockey, compared to 30 percent in Bantam and Midget.

Other Facts

- Currently there are 1,190 Peewee kids registered with Hockey Calgary.
- Hockey Calgary has 13,200 registered hockey players.
- Hockey Calgary is the largest minor hockey associations in Alberta.

We challenged Dr. Emery's study. She had compared Calgary to Quebec in the first study, but she
had only given us results from the Peewee age
group. We wanted to see what impact the elimination of body checking in Peewee would have on
the kids once they reached Bantam. We thought
that we might actually be creating a bigger problem by eliminating body checking, because children were bigger at 13 and 14 than they were at
eleven and twelve. So, we challenged her study.
We wanted to see what would happen in Bantam
before we made any recommendations.

Every sport has their problems – there's no question. Whether it is soccer, football, lacrosse, rugby,
or countless other popular sports, they all have injuries in them. But every sport has an obligation to
review what's going on. In the absence of data, I
say to every one of those sports, *go out and get the
data*. Get a data sampling, just as the NFL is now
doing in football; they've put in place the inten-
tional head contact rule, which never used to be in
NFL.

Dr. Emery came back to us two years ago, and she
reviewed the studies with us during our board
meetings. More than fifty scientists worked on the
study, and it is an incredible piece of work.

I asked every question I could think of. And I
couldn't find one single data point pointing
towards the fact that we should allow Peewee
children to go onto the ice and body check one
another. I couldn't find one.

To knowingly put eleven- and twelve-year-old
boys on the ice, knowing that there's a 33%

greater chance for injury in our hockey environment than Quebec's hockey environment, and that they are going to experience 33% more major injuries, is moronic.

How can we change the rules of hockey so quickly? I'll tell you how it can work.

1. Simply ban body checking in Peewee, making it a foul, just as it is in Atom, the age category below Peewee. We would save an approximate annual number of 500 serious injuries in Calgary alone.

2. Give kids leaving Peewee and entering Bantam level hockey better instructions. Always give kids two practices to every game. And dedicate at least a third of every practice to teaching Peewee players in a safe environment how to body check, helping them to build up their skills and knowledge of body checking as the year progresses.

3. Teach them about the dangers of open-ice body checking. Unfortunately, the NHL and sports broadcasts have glamorized big open-ice hits that leave someone motionless on the ice. I don't think anyone gets a

thrill out of seeing children motionless on the ice as a result of such an aggressive hit.

4. Become informed. Do the research. There are hundreds of readily available books and articles on this topic. There are also many experts, scientists, and doctors that are prepared to come and talk to you about this. It's a matter of getting educated. Unfortunately, if you don't do step 4, in terms of education and getting informed, then you're going to run into another problem. The numbers of kids in minor hockey will continue to diminish. Talk to your hockey branch, and Hockey Canada. They have tremendous resources available, and are readily available to help.

Although the ban on Peewee body checking was voted down in our Hockey Calgary organization, I applaud what's going on in the United States right now. USA Hockey has taken out Peewee body checking across the board, end of discussion (link to the video: http://bit.ly/usa-body-check). I hope that will happen in Canada someday soon as well.

For the life of me, I can't imagine that any child wants to be exposed to more danger because they love body checking so much. I've watched too many frightened young children lying on the ice in tears after being hit by a brutal, legal body check.

I can't think of any environment where parents would allow that to happen without a sense of trepidation. Quite frankly, if such an environment exists, I suspect we should be calling child welfare, not talking to the hockey association.

I challenge everyone, on both sides of the debate, to do research and become informed. As a result of getting informed, let your voice be heard.

Many have spoken up in different ways, but they have been met with resistance, and too many have given up. We cannot give up anymore.

Speak up, let your voice be heard, and get your message out to your hockey associations. There are many ways you can do that, from petitioning to simply attending general annual meetings and board meetings. Get involved as a volunteer, and stand up for a cause that is all about child safety.

Most importantly, if you are a parent, talk to your child, and encourage others to do the same. See if your child feels comfortable in every situation. Do they feel like they have a *Magic Helmet* on when they are on the ice rink, or do they enjoy the sport?

People at the highest levels of minor hockey have said to me, "Body checking is part of our game, it's the way it should be, and it's the way it's always been." They have said, "It's the game of *hockey* – of course kids are going to get hurt! It's just part of the game!"

No. It doesn't have to be that way. You are wrong.

That's the kind of logic that made people think that "buckling up" in a car wasn't "cool." Unfortunately, if you don't wear a seat belt, you might just get thrown through the front windshield of your car.

Take off the *Moron Helmet*. Everything will start making a lot more sense.

Chapter Three
CONCUSSIONS

A 16-year-old boy in a high level Midget game was crossing the rink, mid-ice, going into the zone with the puck. He had his head down. He was body checked by a defender square in the chest, but with such force it knocked him over. His helmet bounced on the ice with a thud.

A hockey helmet is designed to protect the skull. It's not there to protect the brain. So, when you think about this teenager whose head bounced on the ice, the helmet did a perfect job. It protected his skull. There was no blood, the skull wasn't cracked, and it seemed that all injury had been averted. But that player had an internal injury.

This young man shared with me after his game that he had no knowledge of the next three shifts that he played. No knowledge at all.

So, when this 16-year-old, playing a game that he loves, went to the bench after his gigantic hit on the ice, he mumbled to the other players, "Oh yeah, I took a big hit on my head." The kid's head had rebounded off the ice like a marble, and yet he started on each of the next three shifts. Everyone thought everything was fine.

Only at the end of the game, did the kid say to his father, "My head's still sore." At that point, his dad decided to take him to the hospital. Fortunately, he was diagnosed, and sat out numerous games after that. His parents were smart, and said, "Hey, you're going to be benched; you're not going to play for a while."

Doctors now say that, after a concussion, it's not good enough just to refrain from playing hockey or other physical activity. People also shouldn't play things like X-Box or other video games that stimulate the brain in any way.

This 16-year-old can only handle another two concussions if in fact he hasn't already had some, according to several studies. We still don't know the long-term implications. Where does he go if he has had another concussion or two, and what will happen to his cognitive learning abilities as time goes on? What will happen to the wellness of his brain as it relates to that?

When I was a kid, if you had a concussion, Mom or Dad might come in, check you every hour or two at night in order to make sure that you were only sleeping, weren't vomiting, and hadn't gone into a coma.

Medicine has advanced by leaps and bounds over the decades since then, but unfortunately, the safety of the game has not. In other words, we're still allowing body checking, and one of the major outcomes of a body check is a concussion in minor sports. In addition to that, we're still having conversations on the bench that sound just like what I heard as a kid: "Oh, you just got your bell rung. Don't worry about it – it should be okay!"

The problem with a concussion is that kids don't tell you. Players don't tell you. It's never even discussed. 90 percent of concussions go undetected, and new evidence suggests that the healing time is longer for youths than adults. Add to that the little understood issue of longer-term symptoms that crop up in adults in their 40's and 50's, and you have a potential time bomb.

A concussion is a quiet kind of injury that is not like a broken arm where the bone's sticking out of the jersey, or you can't move your arm and there's blood all over the place so we've got to get you to the hospital. Who's to know, if the player doesn't tell you how they are feeling?

After a concussion happens, you can't see inside the head, there's no visible trauma on the outside of the head, the helmet's not cracked, the player got up after getting hit – he might have shaken his head a couple of times and the coach or trainer might have turned to the player and said, "Hey, are you okay?" Or, if a player is lucky enough to have a trainer on the bench, the trainer might have actually looked in his eyes and not seen the pupils dilating, and since the kid isn't vomiting on the bench, the trainer sends him back out to play, even though he might be concussed.

Then the player gets concussed again and again and again, and there's all kinds of evidence again that the repetitive aspect of concussions is exponential.

When I was a kid, we didn't understand the long-term implications of bruising of the brain. A concussion is something like having a bruise on your arm, but you can't see it because you are wearing a leather jacket over it all the time. In the case of the brain, you never know. You have that big thing called a skull surrounding it, thank goodness, but then it's very difficult to see when you've been concussed.

The following is a great guide written by the MediResource clinical team about concussions (reprinted here with permission).

8 things you should know about concussion

1. What is a concussion?

A concussion is a brain injury that can temporarily alter the way the brain functions. When jarred or shaken, the soft tissue of the brain can move around inside the skull and knock into the hard bone. Bruising, torn blood vessels, and nerve damage can result.

2. What causes a concussion?

A concussion is often caused by a blow to the head. A person might suffer a concussion due to a fall, injuries resulting from a car accident, or any number of types of impact injuries, like a hard tackle in football or a high-hit or body-check in hockey.

3. What are the symptoms of a concussion?

Concussion symptoms range from unconsciousness to no outward symptoms at all. The most common immediate symptoms include confusion, dizziness, amnesia, ringing in the ears, and headache. Speech may be slurred, and the person may vomit or feel nauseated or fatigued. Over the course of hours or days, other symptoms may emerge: memory or concentration problems, sleep disturbances, changes in mood, and sensitivity to light and to sound. In many cases, the symptoms of concussion resolve after treatment and rest.

4. Do a child's symptoms of concussion differ from an adult's?

A very young child may not be able to explain their symptoms, so adults should watch for signs of listlessness, unsteadiness, or changes in a child's mood or patterns of eating or sleeping. A child should be closely monitored during the hours and days following a concussion. Ask a health care provider for more information about the signs to watch for and any special instructions to protect your child during recovery.

5. What should you do if you suspect a concussion?

Seek immediate medical attention for a person who has lost consciousness, is vomiting or having seizures, or is showing signs of obvious mental difficulty. If a person does not lose consciousness, a "better safe than sorry" approach is prudent, since how a head trauma will progress is impossible to predict. Children are especially vulnerable to head injury, so seek medical attention for anything beyond a light bump on the head. A person suspected of having a concussion should never be given aspirin, ibuprofen, or other non-steroidal anti-inflammatory medications, as this can increase the risk of bleeding.

6. How is a concussion treated?

The doctor will examine the person to assess their symptoms, checking pupil size and asking questions to determine extent of confusion and memory loss. Further testing may be ordered, such as a CT scan, EEG, or MRI. Depending on the severity of the concussion, a patient may be told to rest (including rest from the computer or video games) and given medication to deal with headaches or pain. Once the symptoms of concussion have resolved, you can slowly ease back into activities as directed by your doctor.

7. Are there any complications of a concussion?

Symptoms of concussion may linger for months or longer after injuries have healed. In post-concussion syndrome, a person may continue to experience headaches, dizziness, fatigue, and changes in mood, sleep, and memory. Repeated concussions may lead to permanent neurological damage.

8. How can a concussion be prevented?

A concussion most often happens by accident, and not all causes can be prevented. To reduce your risk, protect yourself and your family from the most common dangers. Wear a seat belt whenever

you ride in a car. Strap children in to age- and
size-appropriate safety seats. Wear protective gear
whenever engaged in sports or active pursuits that
pose injury risks (skating, bicycling, horseback rid-
ing, etc.) Wear sensible shoes to prevent slips and
falls.

Everything goes back to respect. When players
have an opportunity to perform a big open-ice
body check, they should consciously ease up. You
don't need to do it. There's no benefit other than
stoking the moronic yells, screams, and cheers
from people in the stands.

From a player's perspective, it's important to always play with respect. Play with the attitude that
you will never go out there and hurt someone.
Why would you want to see somebody's head
bouncing off the ice?

In terms of the player who is hurt, we need to re-
define what "toughness" is. Being tough doesn't
have to mean "sucking it up" and not telling people when we're hurt. When you're hurt in a game
of hockey, whether your shoulder is hurt, or your
knee is acting up, or in this case, you had a brain
injury, you need to stand up and make sure that
people are aware of that.

I get most sensitive when I talk about kids, because
we need to educate them that it's important for

them to share their feelings with parents, coaches and volunteers. It's important to tell the coach, "I don't remember playing my last three shifts," or, "I can see spots, my head is sore, I'm feeling dizzy, I feel nauseated." These are the things that are very important, if a child is to continue playing hockey for a lifetime. Every volunteer, including coaches, parents and officials, has a responsibility to teach our children the proper behaviour – and that includes talking about their injuries in an open and honest way.

Look, this is pretty simple. Johnny's head bounces on the ice. Even though he gets back up and seems relatively normal, the coach should openly and honestly ask him whether everything is okay. Then, even if Johnny says he is okay, the coach should probably make the determination that Johnny won't play the rest of the game – just to be sure.

At the end of that game, the coach should go to Johnny's mother and father, and say, "Look, you probably notice little Johnny was sitting out during the game because he hit his head really hard. I think it's important that you get him to the hospital to be evaluated."

Hockey Canada has done a good job of making sure that this kind of information is available to coaches and parents, but the underlying culture still discourages kids from reporting when they have been injured.

Most importantly, parents need to take a larger role in Johnny's well-being, and when he hits his head on the ice, they need to ask him if he's all right. It's better to be safe than sorry, and if you think that Johnny might have the risk of any kind of brain trauma, professional assessment is a must.

Hockey is dangerous in many ways, and concussions have been part of the game for a long time. Having said that, parents, players, and coaches all need to take the responsibility of monitoring player's well-being. So, what do we do when concussions happen?

The worst thing to do is nothing. If Johnny gets a concussion and doesn't talk about it, that is probably the worst-case scenario. So, we need to make sure that we utilize our communication skills as coaches, volunteers, and parents, and we need to be more attentive while talking with Johnny, working hard to understanding the severity of his potential injury. If we don't know how bad the concussion is, or what the consequences might be, we need to keep in mind that this is a fun game, and these are young kids. We let Johnny sit out for a game or two, so that we can monitor him and see how he's doing. Even if he's a great player, we shouldn't risk putting him out on the ice, because it could cause drastic complications in his life. The only cure for concussion is total elimination of the activity for a period of time.

I have a friend who's an ex NHL player, and today, he admits that he "messed up" his head as a result of all the concussions he suffered throughout his minor and pro career. More players are coming out into the public with their stories of brain damage every day. Do we want our kids to tell that same story?

When I think about all the different parties that share responsibility in the case of concussions, it makes me think that we still have work to do. Governing bodies are generally doing their job in terms of the education process, putting in place tools that coaches, parents and kids can use to prevent and detect concussions.

However, we must go further than that. We have to go through an education of parents, players, and coaches, so that we stop saying things like, "Don't worry about it, suck it up," or "You just got your bell rung." We need to do a better job of explaining to children, and to one another, what the implications of a brain injury can be.

The game's not perfect, and there are plenty of things that require improvement inside the game. Having said that, I will venture to say (as I did in the Preface) that 95 percent of activities and behaviours are great. Ninety-five percent of the parents behind the glass are very respectful, cheering enthusiastically, and acting like good, standup citizens. On the ice, 95 percent of the time, body checks don't cause any major damage to kids. Ninety-five percent of kids will never get concussed, or suffer mental illness problems as a result of minor hockey.

However, at the end of the day, just because 95 percent of the game is functional doesn't mean that the sport is healthy. A five-percent failure rate is not like getting 95/100 on a test. It's not an "A" grade. Instead, it's nearly a failing grade. It's a failing grade. If three percent of our kids get concussions that very well may lead to lifelong brain damage, we are failing them, and we need to change something. We can't ignore this problem. We have to stand up, get involved, and start altering the five percent figure.

Imagine only five percent of the people on your street were pedophiles. How would you feel? Safe, because 95 percent were *not* pedophiles? Why are we okay with a five percent rate of failure when it comes to the safety of our kids in hockey?

Until our kids are 100 percent safe, parents need to stand up, coaches need to stand up, all of the custodians of the game need to stand up, and all of us need to make sure that we are making the game as safe as it possibly can be.

THE BEHIND THE SCENES STORY OF MINOR HOCKEY

PART TWO:
THE POLICY

Chapter Four
FAIR PLAY

After 99 years of our children playing minor hockey in Canada, there are plenty of rules, regulations, processes, and policies in place to govern all aspects of the game – particularly around the issue of "fair play". If everyone were to follow these policies, we would have a pretty good system in place.

When it comes to how players, coaches, parents, officials, spectators and league organizers behave, there are clear rules and codes as to what is acceptable behaviour and what is unacceptable behaviour. It would be a beautiful world if everyone obeyed these fair play behaviours. The problem is that these rules and codes are ultimately not adhered to. In minor hockey, we need to remember that our first priority is to keep our children safe, having a good time, respecting one another, and playing in an environment where they are able to learn the great game of hockey.

Human nature all too often messes up the balance of our beloved sport. Suddenly, there are 19 kids on the hockey team, and coaches leave the "worst" player on the bench, even though that player probably needs the most experience and development. Those coaches make a clear distinction between their "best" and "worst" hockey line, using that information to win the hockey game. By keeping only the best players out on the ice, they are violating the rules of minor hockey. The best coaches say, "I'm going to be the guy who makes sure that all kids develop equally. I'm going to make sure that all kids get equal ice time." Coaches need to be committed to equal participation and equal development for all players and for the betterment of the game.

For many coaches, parents and people on the sidelines, the focus of this kids' game is on the almighty win. Hockey is almost a religion in Canada, and winning is paramount in many of these adults' minds. That has to change, if we are to teach our children to enjoy the game, and if we are to eliminate bullying and other damaging practices. We can never forget that the basic principle of minor hockey is the development of children.

Kids should get equal play, support, and instruction. That's the rules, and it's what is right for our young hockey players. Coaches should not yell at their young players, or ridicule them for making mistakes or performing poorly. They need to remember that their players play to have fun, and should encourage them to have confidence in themselves.

I was recently a linesman for a Peewee provincial hockey game. As a linesman, I am often in clear earshot of the coaches as they shout directions to their players. I was sickened by what I heard during this particular game. The coach in question screamed continuously at these Peewee children. He was clearly shortening the bench, and rotating his "best" players every second shift. He swore angrily, and shouted that they shouldn't be "babies." Their team was winning by two goals at that point. I wonder what happens when they are losing.

The goal of minor hockey is not to prime kids for NHL play (that is a happy by-product for a very small minority of players). Instead, the goal is to develop their personalities, skills, and self-esteem. The most important thing an adult, whether a coach, parent, official, spectator, or league organizer, can do around children is model the best behaviour, and set a good example. These kids spend an awful lot of time with these adults, and they are very impressionable.

We have a major problem in minor hockey. We are further from fair play than ever before, and it has nothing to do with the kids. It's our fault, and our responsibility, as adults. There are a few reasons we are not doing very well at this.

It used to be that parents actually had to sign the fair play policies when they signed up their child for playing minor hockey in Canada. Today, parents just click on a little box on the online registration saying, "I have read the attached." Unfortunately, not many have actually read the policies or are aware of them. In countless conversations with involved adults, I have asked them about the fair play policy, and whether or not they are aware of it. Most have no idea that there's even a code in place. Although it's not an easy fix, we need to make sure that responsible adults actually read the paperwork, so that they can obey and enforce the fair play policies.

For easy reference, here is the Hockey Calgary version of the Fair Play Policy, posted on their website, and in their rules and regulations. Your hockey association will have a similar policy, as this comes down from Hockey Canada.

FAIR PLAY CODE POLICY FOR COACHES

The fair play codes are set out in Hockey Canada's booklet Safety Requires Teamwork – An information guide to Hockey Canada's Risk Management and National Insurance Programs. The fair play codes are a set of guidelines for players, coaches, parents, officials, spectators and league organizers set out to promote positive hockey experiences. Fair play is important from a developmental perspective as well as from a risk management perspective.It is the policy of the Hockey Calgary that the Fair Play Codes be followed by all member associations affiliated with Hockey Calgary including AA, Community, Girls Hockey, Recreational Hockey and High School Hockey. For the most part the fair play codes are clear. However, for coaches there is a provision, which states, "I will ensure that all players get equal instruction, support and playing time." The use of the term "equal" is generally understood. However, there is a tendency among a small minority to misinterpret the term "equal" with "earned" or "fair" which allows for entirely different interpretations of the intentions of the fair play codes. Some individuals will acknowledge that the fair play codes apply and then claim you can shorten the bench in the last five minutes of a game, in a tight situation or in playoffs. Allowing variances in the interpretation of fair play only increases a broader degree of confusion for the rules of minor hockey. Fair play is intended to allow all players an equal opportunity to develop their skills in Hockey. Development occurs in both practice and game situations. And within the game itself, there are different situations where each player should be afforded the opportunity to develop his or her skills, whether it is power play, penalty kill, playoffs or tournaments. The following policy respecting ice time is intended to ensure a consistent application of the fair play codes throughout the Hockey Calgary network with an emphasis to ensure all players are provided equal opportunity to develop his or her hockey skills in every game situation. The policy applies to AA Hockey, Community Hockey, Girls Hockey, Recreational Hockey and High School Hockey.

When I was a Board Member with Hockey Calgary, I had a group of parents approach me after a hockey game in which one line of kids didn't see nearly as much ice time as the "elite" line. On this occasion, I decided to address this with this coach. I talked to him before his next game, asking him about the fair play complaint raised by parents.

The coach said, "Look, it's my hockey team. I'm going to move the lines how I want to move them and I'm going to play the kids who I think are playing the best." For added emphasis, he reiterated, "That's who I'm going to play."

In my role with Hockey Calgary, I needed to explain to him that this wasn't his right, and that the children fell beneath the fair play policies of our organization. His job was to develop all players equally, and give them equal playing time.

He didn't agree with me. So we watched his games carefully over the following weeks, and saw as he allowed an entire line of kids to sit on the bench for the entire game. This behaviour was moronic, and it was our responsibility to watch out for the children he was mistreating. Not to give this any more airtime than he deserves, but the issue was dealt with, and the coach was suspended by Hockey Calgary for his actions.

The real answer is for everyone to stand up and hold others accountable for moronic behaviour. If your child's coach is acting like Spider-Man, or like the screaming coach above, you need to stand up. Adults can't ignore this kind of behaviour. Unfortunately, this is not as easily done as one might think. Parents and others won't speak up because they believe their kids won't get equal play if the coach doesn't like them – so they stay silent. It's not worth it; speak up!

Remember, your child's eyes and ears are on you, and on every adult around you. Watching and listening to every behaviour. Are you accepting wrong behaviour out of fear of retaliation? It's time to stop the cycle of bullying.

The most important thing is the education process. Adults should not simply assume that their natural upbringing or basic skills that they have learned inside of their own lives are the ones that should be adhered to inside of minor sports. Membership in minor sports is a privilege, not a right, and the rules need to be followed. In other words, it's not a God-given right that suddenly you're born and you're permitted to play organized hockey. Each adult and child has a role to play, and appropriate behaviours to follow:

- We ask players to understand how they have to behave, and how they have to play.

- We should also make sure coaches know their role, and act appropriately. Parents, you have a role in this as well. You are not just writing the cheque to allow your son to play. You need to understand the game, the rules, the regulations, and what would be best for your child.

- I don't want to let officials off the hook either. I have witnessed officials who had not been given the right training or mentoring, and didn't act appropriately either. If you are a referee, remember your role. It is not just for the couple of bucks that you are getting paid. We are counting on you!

- Spectators, whether siblings, grandparents, or parents, also have a responsibility in terms of what their behaviour looks like. What do they say to players and officials on the ice? Are they just cheering and getting excited, or are they bullying people from the stands?

- The league organizers are also responsible to behave appropriately. Your decision to volunteer does not give you veto power or the ability to ignore the rules. You are the caretaker of the rules as they are written. And everyone needs to be held accountable. No free rides!

The biggest concern I have for minor hockey is the parents. Yes, kids bully one another in the locker room and elsewhere, but they have learned that behaviour from someone else. It is the parents who more often bully one another or the kids, and this is behaviour their children follow. The more we close our eyes to it, and the more we just accept it as a byproduct of the game, the more we are neglecting our duty to the children in minor hockey.

At one general meeting when we were discussing the problems in minor hockey, one older man in his late 60's, who had been around Hockey Canada his entire life, said, "It has always been that way." I fully respect him for all his years of volunteerism, but his comment was unacceptable to me. He implied that, since "it has always been that way," it will "always be that way" in the future. I don't ascribe to that point of view. I believe that, if we insist that all adults in the minor hockey system simply started taking accountability and read the fair play code, working hard to abide by its rules and regulations, we would be 99% on our way towards fixing the problems that exist in the game today.

When I talk to leaders these days, as part of my executive coaching work, I ask them about their upbringing playing in minor sports – in particular, hockey. They tell me things like, "Boy, I made so many great friends, and I had so many great memories, and so many tremendous things happened." They remember traveling to hockey tournaments, going to team parties, and playing a sport with all of their best friends. These successful individuals honestly do not talk about the season they won all of the games, or scored the most goals, and they don't bring up where they finished in the standings.

Ultimately, it's about playing the game of hockey that I love, and that we all love. But we have to remember, especially at the Atom and Peewee level, it's just a game, and it's about children developing skills, talents, and relationships. If we can remember that, our kids will win after every game, regardless of the tally of "wins" and "losses."

Chapter Five
THE RULES

The rules of minor hockey have evolved over time. Hockey Canada has been very conscientious of continually improving the game from a participant level as well as from a spectator level with respect to speed and excitement. For example, it used to be that the game was much more of a clutch-and-grab game – where people would grab onto you while you were skating by them. That started to be called "hooking" and was outlawed. Years ago, a stop sign was placed on the back of every minor hockey player's jersey, and rule emphasis was placed on not hitting players from behind.

Recently, Hockey Canada has started to make several changes with regard to safety. One of those changes is that they have put in place a head contact rule. Previous to this rule change, players would receive a two-minute minor penalty, and a ten-minute misconduct penalty. At face value, that sounds significant – and it was. The real problem was that on-ice officials weren't necessarily calling the penalty, because of how such an infraction could influence one player by taking him out of the game for ten minutes. What ended up happening is that, as a result, the hit-to-the-head call was not being called as often as it should have been. Two years ago, any direct contact to the helmet (or head) instead became a four-minute minor penalty, and accidental contact to the head was a two-minute minor penalty. If there was an injury as a result, the official could increase that to a major penalty. That rule has had more success than any single change in the last decade. The head is *not* in play. Great job, Hockey Canada!

Everything is in place to have a tremendously successful organization, and for children to have a fantastic and safe experience inside of minor hockey. But, at the end of the day, people have to follow and abide by the policies for the rules to function.

Ultimately, minor hockey is not about the rules — it's about the kids having fun, learning life and leadership skills, and learning to exercise and socialize. But without proper rules and enforcement of those rules, the kids won't have a safe environment to have fun within.

One example of a situation (where rules are necessary in order to keep the "fun" in hockey for kids) is in the regulation of so-called "elite" category. The idea behind this age category is to assemble Peewee, Bantam, and Midget athletes who are presumably the "best." These children would arguably have the greatest chance to advance to amateur JR, post-secondary school careers, or even professional status.

An old practice in this category used to be to have a recruitment plan where you could invite certain excellent young players to a team and "stack the team." Certain coaches would geographically move elite young athletes to their area. They would go and "recruit" young children to play for their particular community center so that they would have the best team. As a result of this practice, hockey Boards have had to develop rules that tell you when you can and cannot play in a particular community. Remember, this is minor hockey, and no Stanley Cup is on the line here. This is all just about children playing a game. But many adults take this way too seriously, to the detriment of their children.

I had many parents come in to me and ask if their child could move to a particular team, but that was simply not our policy. But, come hell or high water, those parents are going to find a way to move their child from one community to another. In several cases, people have even gone and purchased another house and claimed it to be their primary residence, so that their son could register for a certain hockey team. When we went back and checked a few of these, the family hadn't actually moved to that house, and it was not their primary residence at all – they were renting it. But others purchased a home to "benefit" their son's minor hockey "career." What is wrong with this system?

Hockey Calgary is North America's largest hockey association, with around 4,500 volunteers. They are all giving up a portion of their free time outside of their working careers, domestic chores and all other priorities in life. How much education have they received, and how effective is the organization in getting the correct information to those volunteers? How can we confront systemic problems with this many volunteers?

One word: education. When adults violate the rules, or when they teach young, impressionable players to break the rules, they are jeopardizing all of the children in our care. We need to have a better education process with our volunteers.

When we first earned our driver's license, we had to pass a test. We had to go over a few hurdles in order to earn the right, and have the privilege to drive an automobile. Yet, when I think about volunteers, we just naturally assume that everyone gets it – there is no such test to earn the right to work with the kids in minor hockey. The organization takes it for granted that all individuals will go off and read the appropriate documents behind the scenes on their own, and they will be able to comprehend and put them to practice.

We will talk more about volunteers in later chapters, but suffice to say, there is no prerequisite for getting involved in minor hockey in a volunteer capacity, and there isn't much required training. In fact, there's no disciplined orientation program. We just take for granted that everyone is going to do the right thing. And what ends up happening is that most volunteers do a great job, but a significant, small minority of poor volunteers creates major systemic problems.

For the most part, kids are not the problem, because they understand the rules. When the whistle blows, the official will put little Johnny into the penalty box, and he'll sit there for the next two minutes. However, coaches, spectators, parents, and others don't feel the same relationship to the rules (coaches in particular). Let's think back to the situation in the last chapter where a 35-year-old coach bullies a twelve-year-old referee. Section 9.2 of the Hockey Canada Rulebook has an entire section dedicated to abuse of officials by coaches. We all need to know the rules, and enforce them when it comes to adults, just as we enforce the rules on our young players during the course of the game.

As a spectator going to an NHL hockey game, you don't have to know all the rules of the game. You can go and watch the puck fly, players fight one another, and join in with the crowd, cheering, jeering and so forth. But we hold a different responsibility when it comes to minor hockey.

It is our responsibility to spend some time with the rulebook. Imagine that you are learning a new card game, or studying to pass a driver's test. Do you really know the rules of the game? Will you know when the coach, a spectator, or an official is breaking the rules?

What is acceptable, and what is not acceptable in terms of playing the game? If you want to be a good custodian of the game, and help our children develop socially and physically in a safe environment, get involved, get engaged, and most importantly, get educated. And when it comes to the rules, learn all of them. Take an active interest with the young hockey players, whether your own children or players in your charge.

Ignorance of the rules and regulations is a major problem. It causes many of the outbursts by people who think officials have made a bad call. It also creates many abrasive and difficult situations within and between teams when parents, coaches, and league officials haven't read the rules. If you are going to play this game or participate at any level, read the rules. Not just the playing rules, but also the regulations; this is a membership-based sport, and there are regulations that pertain to membership – read them!

At the end of the day, what this all comes down to is, we're talking about children from the ages of six to 18. They are on the ice to learn camaraderie, gain some skills, work with coaches, organizers, and officials in a respectful way, and ultimately, just have fun playing the incredible sport of hockey.

Chapter Six
THE STRUCTURE

The structure and hierarchy of hockey in Canada contains an interesting duality. One one hand, hockey is big business. On the other, the entire system of minor hockey in Canada is run by thousands of volunteers.

The game of hockey has come a long way from its beginning on small ponds of ice. It has in many ways been transformed into salaries and profits; just think of the recent lockout in the NHL.

Let's be real about this, Hockey Canada makes money. I believe the reported revenue for the IIHF World Junior Tournament in Calgary was around $20 million dollars. This is a big money-making machine.

All the branches in the minor hockey system have plenty of infrastructure, and each generates huge amounts of cash. The strange thing is, the local minor hockey associations and community clubs are run by volunteers. They *don't* make money. (Or, I should say, they *shouldn't* make money. I am aware of some of these organizations sitting on large excess pools of cash; running huge surpluses every year.)

The entire system is a very large machine that is making some serious errors because certain parts of the structure are generating excess revenues, while others are barely getting by, and relying on the service of dedicated volunteers (who are not being compensated at all).

So, we have got this big machine called Hockey Canada. They have this massive rulebook for us to follow, and then we also have branches found in each province of Canada that sit between Hockey Canada and local minor hockey associations. And then we have the leagues that fit into this mess. The provincial branches have a rulebook. The local minor hockey associations have a rulebook. The leagues all have rulebooks. All of these rules are presumably followed with the help of a few paid staff members and a veritable army of volunteers. So with all these rules, and all these regulations, my goodness, why the heck do we have a problem?

Well, the core problem inside of the whole discussion is that we have volunteer-based organizations spread across North America, where every single one of these communities have dedicated volunteers that are trying their best and are armed with the right tools. But they are not given the right orientation, and they are not educated in terms of what exactly the rules and regulations are, and they are by and large left to "just do the best you can." And "the best you can" creates a pile of problems for the organization and the kids.

I don't want this to come across as if I'm beating up on volunteerism. I'm a big advocate of volunteerism. The issue is that, inside the structure that minor hockey has created, the machine demands a great deal of energy from volunteers, yet the machine does not provide all the guiding principles, orientation, and education that the volunteers need. In other words, the system is flawed from the top down.

A bunch of employees with Hockey Canada are putting great policies in place, but the struggle is that ten percent is the idea, and 90% is the execution of that idea. In this case, not spending enough time with the volunteers is the problem: making sure you have the right volunteers, that they are motivated by the right behaviours, and that they are doing the right jobs. For example, there should be employees (not volunteers) doing important systemic jobs, such as scheduling ice time. At present, volunteers run the majority of the system that operates all aspects of the day-to-day operations as best they can, based on the rules set up by the structure, and as you travel across the structure, there is no consistency. Those with certain skills get more organized than those who do not have those same skills.

Many of the decisions as to how things operate are left up to the direction of volunteers, which inherently can never work as efficiently as when paid staff take care of infrastructure. Additionally, efficiencies are lacking in many areas due to lack of knowledge: volunteers have great intentions, but a lack of knowledge as to how to execute.

I realize that increasing the number of paid roles would increase the cost of the game if there were incremental increases. However, I'm suggesting a complete review and redeployment of roles and responsibilities. In other words, Hockey Canada and branches alike would take more roles and control of critical aspects of their operation, and appropriately reallocate roles managed by volunteers more effectively and efficiently. The general theme is that more volunteers should do less work, while paid infrastructure staff should handle all mission-critical responsibilities.

My goal is not to bad-mouth Hockey Canada or the structure at large. It's a widely successful organization, and has done incredible things for the game of hockey. It would be great if solutions would come from the top down, and specifically, a major overhaul of roles, responsibilities, and infrastructure, but it's probably not going to happen anytime soon. The game started from grassroots, and the core successes have resulted from the great and selfless service of volunteers. And the machinery of minor hockey *does* listen to the masses.

Changes need to come both from the bottom up and the top down.

From the bottom up, if we educate our volunteers properly, and work hard to adhere to the rules that Hockey Canada has put in place, the game will be healthy for years to come. The irony is that the rules and regulations are already all in place.

From the top down, the game needs to be protected by structure. The top structure and general infrastructure is there, but there needs to be a corporate identity threaded throughout the system. We have top-notch professionals running the top end, but we have misguided, misinformed, and in some cases ill-equipped volunteers at the bottom end.

It's time for a reallocation of funding and an implementation of greater control throughout the system. I'm not suggesting the elimination of the volunteer. That would be ridiculous, and not a viable option. But those volunteers need to be more disciplined and controlled. If we don't make that change, we will not gain full awareness of the pockets of incompetence and deceit. The problem is at the grassroots, local level, and the solution is to allow top down to gain greater influence and impact. The top is where the expertise and money is. They already set the rules of the game. Let them implement more of the management before its too late. Along with the bottom up changes, educating our volunteers and rooting out corruption, we will be able to make minor hockey in Canada a viable, long-term, safe, sustainable, and healthy pastime.

MORON

THE BEHIND THE SCENES STORY OF MINOR HOCKEY

PART THREE:

THE CARETAKERS

Chapter Seven
ELITE SYSTEM

We need to make a few serious changes in minor hockey. One of the places that most needs change is the "elite system." Our best athletes and their parents are being disrespected and bullied at the highest level, and we have to start moving in the right direction.

You have 13,500 kids playing the game of hockey inside of the city limits of Calgary, and that story is multiplied times every association across North America. We have basically two types of players: the community player and the more skilled player, who ends up trying out for the "elite system." Elite players are grouped into teams all across Canada. These teams then play around the province. They travel in buses, and they get preferential treatment; they are the cream of the crop. These kids are handpicked through a try-out process in Calgary, ending up at one of 28 elite teams in two different categories, Bantam and Midget.

In fairness, one could argue, "Why do you do that kind of tiering?" The answer is, we are always trying to create an environment where all kids feel like they can go out and participate equally, and that's the reason behind the tiering. Imagine joining a coed volleyball team. You wouldn't want to go out with a bunch of guys who were ex-Olympians, right? You'd want to go with guys who were of similar skill set to yourself.

The elite system in minor hockey is very "elitist." You basically see the opportunity for young players to participate at a highly competitive level on a province-wide basis. They get to travel around. They get to have the experience of an upper echelon athlete with arguably the best coaches in the system for developing the players. They have trainers around them, and they get all the gear, traveling around in this elite structure. The advantages and the experience that a child can gain can be wonderful: a time they will never forget. However, other children may want to forget.

It is very difficult to make the team. It's kind of cruel if you think about it. I've seen this one hundred times over with kids that try out. Anybody can go and try out for the team, but they go through a process of four ice times and they break you down into different teams and you have a little exhibition play and the coaches are all gathered around the arenas and watching all the kids play. It is a process of elimination. Every night, you find out whether your name stays on the list and whether you're still being considered as one of the elite athletes. One wonderful day, you discover that your name is on the particular team.

When my son, T.J., was a lower level Peewee player, he said to me, "Dad, I want to one day become an elite hockey player."

I thought to myself at that time, *Boy that's a stretch.* But of course, I didn't want to burst his bubble or be the dream crasher, right? I thought, *Boy, you're going to have to work pretty hard at that.* And you know? To his credit, he did.

T.J. worked hard. He went to lots of training camps, was very attentive to the coaches, and really worked hard on his development. Obviously, one day he finally made the cut and he was on the Minor Midget AAA team. It was a great achievement for him. So, I know what it's like to be a proud parent of a kid in elite hockey. From that perspective, and having seen the entire thing from the top down as President of Hockey Calgary, I saw the beauty in the elite system, but I also very clearly saw the flaws.

The biggest problem with the elite system is that it's filled with elitists. You have a bunch of individuals (volunteers) that are operating the organization from a top down perspective, and you've got volunteer-based organizations that have somehow decided over time that they are above all the laws and rules. They feel like they can do whatever the heck they want. They think they don't have to adhere to fair play policies. They're not about developing young boys in game of hockey. They are there for all the almighty "win" – and the rules be damned.[5]

They justify their behaviour with the statement, "We're the elite – we operate under different rules." They believe that it's a privilege to have *our* kid on *their* hockey team, and they don't want anyone telling them about what the rules and regulations are (not even their governing body).

While on the sidelines as a parent, I've seen this first hand. I've witnessed coaches, line after line, violating the fair play policy. I've watched coaches become abusive with parents, suggesting to them if they don't quit their whining and complaining, they won't play their children anymore.

I remember one parent coming up to me after a game, saying, "Look, my kid's not even playing. He's just sitting on the bench. The coach isn't allowing my child to play! What can I do?"

I responded to him, "Well, you've got to go up and talk to the coach."

He said, "Well, I can't, because if I talk to the coach, my kid won't be allowed to come back next year."

Really? Okay. So what we're telling our children is, when coaches or other adults break rules, you know what? Just suck it up and do what they say. That's not right.

---

[5] Disclaimer: there were also some *great* coaches and members, but they were unfortunately in the clear minority.

There are no paid coaches in minor hockey. They are all volunteers. However, the elite teams are coached, in some cases, by coaches who consider themselves elite as well. They are supposed to be the best coaches, but they don't always act like it, and put all of their focus on winning, not on developing the players.

We have also had trouble with some of the elite coaches who had received honorariums. That's against the rules, but in the elite level systems, it takes place anyway. Inside of Hockey Calgary, there are 24 smaller hockey associations with their own Boards, including four elite associations. They control their own money, and to the concern of Hockey Calgary, we were discovering that more and more of them had a positive cash flow to the point where they were making substantial profits.

We are not talking about professional status teams. These are kids that are still in the community system. The parents are still spending about $2,500 to $3,000 a year to have their child play the game, and it was becoming clear that excess cash was being accumulated by certain associations. As a member of this system, you should ask to see the financials of your local association.

What often happens is that the "worst" player on the team ends up paying $3000 a year, plus uniforms and other supplies, and he sits on the bench, because the elite coach has decided that Johnny's not playing very well. That is not the way it should be. 19 kids are supposed to get equal development time each game.

One amazing outcome of the elite system in Hockey Canada is that certain players go on to become excellent players in the pros. Very few make it to that level, but there are a few examples. Unfortunately, all parents and coaches involved with the elite teams now cling to those rare stories, further amplifying the problem.

The problem starts at the top. The people who run the elite associations believe that they are above all of the minor hockey rules and regulations, regardless of whether they are elite teams or not. In Hockey Calgary, I have seen a great deal of evidence to support the existence of this problem, and I have also seen the problem myself.

I visited an elite hockey game about a year ago, and was made aware of the fact that a player was playing despite his suspension as a result of a hit-from-behind call made in a previous game. According to Hockey Calgary rules, that player should have missed a game as a result of that dangerous behaviour.

Nevertheless, the player continued to play in the game, and when I questioned team officials, they said they "interpreted the rule" differently than I did.

So, the coach refused to listen, and was now playing an ineligible player, which is probably the worst thing a coach could do inside of any minor sport. He had an ineligible player on the ice.

Team officials were asked several times to act on this blatant rule violation.

I told the coach, calmly, "If you take him off the ice right now, we'll be able to close our eyes to this thing, and you will say you made a mistake, and we'll move on."

They fought me on this, but eventually the player was removed from the ice. From there, they still argued the point that they were exempt from that particular rule. They had their own rules.

In some cases, they also have their own side businesses, and profit from their activities with the elite teams. Certain coaches and elite executive members say to parents, "Only kids who go through a certain training program can come onto our elite team." Parents are easily taken in by these behaviours, because they are looking out for their child's best interest, whatever the cost.

For for the life of me, I don't understand the logic of these elitist coaches and administrators. I don't understand their behaviour. But that kind of behaviour is not unique to Calgary; it's rampant throughout the entire minor hockey system.

Our kids need to not be thought of as future NHL stars, but treated like kids. All 19 players need to have equal time on the ice, and they need to be protected by the same rules that protect all kids in the community hockey system. The rules were enacted to keep our kids safe, regardless of skill or age.

I understand why parents and others are reluctant to get involved. I liken the situation to that of a bully on the street. If you see some kid get bullied across the street, do you do anything, or do you think, "it's none of my business?"

Well, that's just not right. When we see something bad happening, we should be getting involved. We should be stepping up and saying, "Hey, this isn't acceptable."

The masses can get involved, but the movement has to start with one parent, one coach, one spectator, one kid.

But when it comes down to it, there is only one way to overcome the fear and intimidation that exists inside of all of the elite associations. Something has to be done in order to save this side of minor hockey; remember, it *is* minor hockey. The solution is that the elite system needs to be taken down to its foundation, and built again from scratch.

The foundation and rules of the elite system are very sound, and Hockey Canada has a great development model in place. Unfortunately, the elite system (especially in Calgary) has an apparent and blatant disregard for those rules. And the presidents (including me) of Hockey Calgary have all wanted to change things, but were never able to enact significant measures to bring the situation under control.

What we need to do now is to dismantle the system. Using Calgary as the example, we need to take apart all four associations, and put those elite teams directly into Hockey Calgary. It's the only way.

The Board of Hockey Calgary has the power to do this. And it's time for them to simply stand up and say, "Look, enough! We've got to fix this. There's a problem."

The solution is very simple. Bring the elite associations under the banner of Hockey Calgary again – they have strayed too far from the fold. Centralize them, and take care of Calgary's most elite children athletes again. Don't change the rules, but start to enforce them – for the protection of the kids, and the beauty of the game. Then, following this model, minor hockey associations across Canada can embrace this approach.

My experience and knowledge is very specific to Calgary. I understand the problem well in this city, as do many others. I am also privy to the fact that this elite problem is not unique to Calgary. It is a minor hockey problem. The system is fundamentally broken, and we need to work together to fix it.

Chapter Eight
PARENTS, COACHES & OFFICIALS

I grew up in the game of hockey, as did my son, who started playing at the age of five. I remember putting T.J. to bed as a five-year-old, and he wanted to wear his hockey equipment all night long, so that he could get up the next morning and skate with his friends. And I vividly remember my father standing in the crowd for my hockey games as a child, with his black leather gloves, and what I called his "old man hat," always applauding and cheering me on. I understand what it's like to have a loving parent on the sidelines, and I know what it's like to be a dad cheering for his kid.

I have also been a coach for minor hockey since I was a young married man in Winnipeg – before we had children. I coached the Atom age level (ten- to eleven-year-olds) at that point, and I loved every minute of it, even though it could be bitterly cold at times. Many of the games were played in outdoor facilities, and many times the cold Winnipeg winds would whip through the rink with a vengeance.

Although I don't play anymore, my son has moved on from minor hockey, and I no longer coach a team, I still referee many games each season – something I thoroughly enjoy doing, and won't stop anytime soon. Over the last seven years, I have officiated many levels of minor hockey, from Atom all the way up to Junior C (18-20 year-olds).

I think I have a pretty complete picture of what it feels like to walk in the shoes of all three "caretakers" of the game – the adults who have direct contact with kids in minor hockey. I have been a parent, a coach, and an official. So, I don't come at this only from the perspective of someone who has been the president of Hockey Calgary. I am one of the people who love this sport as a pastime and a way of life.

I have been part of some amazing times in each of these three roles, and I would not trade those experiences for the world. When parents, coaches, and officials all work together in synergy, the kids can safely learn and experience the incredible game of hockey to the fullest extent.

I remember very clearly one Atom game within which a coach got out of control and displayed extremely moronic behaviour. This 35-year-old coach's players were nine and ten years old, and the official on the ice was twelve years old (a child, himself). After shouting at the twelve-year-old referee the entirety of the game, the coach not only refused to shake the boy's hand, he belittled, chastised, and shouted at him, to the point that the first-year coach was afraid to go into the dressing room with the other linesmen and referees. The boy sat on the bench in tears until all of the other referees had left the dressing room. Then he quickly went into the locker room, got changed, and waited for his Mom and Dad to pick him up. He was so devastated that he didn't attend school the next day. He was afraid that the other two linesmen would make fun of him because he had made a bad call in a hockey game. This 35-year-old coach had bullied a twelve-year-old so terribly that his life was dramatically impacted.

This particular situation escalated even further when we brought that coach in for a hearing. I was in the room, and I asked the coach, "What were you thinking? Help me understand what's going on here."

The coach responded, "It's not my problem. This is a problem with Hockey Calgary."

When I asked the coach to clarify, he said, "We need to do a better job of teaching our officials how to deal with conflict resolution."

In other words, this 35-year-old coach felt that yelling and screaming at a twelve-year-old boy was appropriate, since the boy had presumably made a bad call in a game for nine- and ten-year-olds. He believed that Hockey Calgary had to do a better job of teaching children (in this case, the twelve-year-old official) to deal with conflict.

Clearly, this adult had other issues.

This coach is the exception to the rule. Most coaches are wonderful role models for our children. But this kind of behaviour is unacceptable around our children, and something has to be done to root out this kind of thing.

Parents, Coaches, and Officials are ultimately responsible for what goes on in minor hockey: they watch over the children to make sure they are safe, and that they don't bully one another, but they should also watch over one another. If all three caretakers make sure that the others fulfill their respective roles, the system will work perfectly.

However, all too often, one of those caretakers starts to go sideways, whether it be the parents yelling and screaming at other players, parents, or on-ice officials, coaches screaming at players or on-ice officials, or on-ice officials screaming back at coaches. If any one of those individuals starts to "lose it," so to speak, you know you end up with a complete mess, and chaos inside the system.

I think, over my time with Hockey Calgary, I have witnessed some of the worst behaviour you could possibly imagine. I already described Spider-Man in a previous chapter, and the mother who fought another woman in the stands. I have described a coach screaming at a young official. I have also witnessed police being called to hockey rinks and escorting parents from the place, and I've seen parents lose it with their own children, screaming at their pre-teen son because of some "bad" play or another.

I'm quite convinced that, if I could show up to the workplace of these individuals, and show them a video of their behaviour, they would probably say, "My goodness, what the heck was I doing? What have I done? Why did I do that?"

I wish more coaches would also reflect on the things they sometimes do in the midst of a situation. I have seen many coaches do what I call the "Don Cherry" at the side of the rink. Don Cherry was an outrageously outspoken coach who would stand up on top of the boards, and he would address the crowd as well as the officials anytime he didn't like a call. In any case, what do these Don Cherrys do in minor hockey? They stand up on the bench, put their foot up there so that they can speak down to players and officials on the ice.

You wouldn't think that coaches would behave this way around the younger kids, but in my experience, this is exactly where this behaviour happens most. For whatever reason, these guys forget that they have young, impressionable eight-year-old children out on the ice, and they lose their sanity, put on their moron helmets and start yelling and screaming about something or another.

In minor hockey, we are always talking about children from five to 18 years old. And, yes, even 18-year-olds are quite impressionable – maybe even more than some of the five-year-olds. It is a shame to see an adult who is now the coach, one of the critical components to the success of the game, yelling and screaming at officials at the top of his lungs, using profanity, and ultimately embarrassing his entire team, often getting ejected from the hockey game by the official.

There are around 26,000 officials across Canada for minor hockey. In Calgary alone, we have just under 1,000 officials to manage all of the hockey that's played throughout a hockey season. Although these officials are getting a couple of dollars, they're certainly not doing it as a career. The young referees are the most excited about a few extra dollars in their pockets – some of them officiating hockey instead of slinging hamburgers at the local fast food joint.

These officials turn around in large quantities every year, because coaches and parents yell at them during and after every game, and it ultimately proves not to be worth it for them. They will make a few mistakes, just as the coaches and parents do, but officials are publicly berated and belittled whenever they have an error in judgment on the ice.

I have also seen the flip side of this. If an official enters the ice with a chip on his shoulder, the game will probably not go well. Officials receive very little training in terms of managing conflict on the ice. In fact, many times the officials are only children themselves.

Ultimately if we focus in on all three caretakers: the parents, the coaches, and the on-ice officials; if they are all better trained, and if there are better programs in place to make sure their behaviours are kept in check, minor hockey will be a much more positive experience for the children.

I've been asked this question many times as the past-president of Hockey Calgary, as well as when I was a hockey parent, a past coach and a present on-ice official. "What is your view of the game? Is the game broken?"

Very simply, I would answer the question by saying, "You know, the game has a Band-Aid on it. And my opinion, there are some serious issues that need to be addressed."

Do the best you possibly can.

Get involved with every level of development that is made available to you, and remember that at the end of the day, you're doing this for children. You owe it to them.

Chapter Nine
VOLUNTEERISM

There are 4,500 volunteers inside the system of minor hockey in Calgary. It's a wonderful thing that minor sports can be run by volunteers. Parents and community members are getting involved in the lives of their kids; what could be wrong with that? The problem only arises when you look at *why* a small percentage of these people volunteer.

Because there is always a need for volunteers, we have become complacent, and if someone puts a hand up and says, "Hey, I want to be a volunteer," they literally get accepted for the role on the spot. Even in the most senior roles in the system, where people are choosing not to be involved for whatever reasons, if a warm body lifts an arm and says, "I'll do it," the association will respond, "Yeah, he's got a pulse. Put him in the job."

This reckless lack of regulation of volunteers in minor hockey is quite frankly the number one problem in the sport.

The way I see it, here is how it breaks down: there are three kinds of volunteers. Let's start with the positive.

Volunteers in Group #1 are there for the right reasons. They have the skills and competencies to do the job they volunteer for, and they show up when they are needed.

Volunteers in Group #2 are there for very different reasons. They are there for the jacket, the badge of honor, or a benefit from their corporation. They literally do nothing. They may have the skills and competencies for the job, but they aren't interested in being involved past what will get them an achievement on their wall or on their resume.

Volunteers in Group #3 are there to make sure that their child always gets an edge. In many cases, their child doesn't want or need their help to achieve that edge. But the parent is there anyway. They say to themselves, "Boy, if I'm on the Board, or the Evaluation Committee, I can make sure that my son, Johnny, will be on the most elite division." The way that works is, if that parent is on a committee that evaluates a certain coach, that coach will make sure that Johnny gets plenty of ice time.

Volunteer #1: There for the right reasons

A man I will call Charles was on the Board of Hockey Calgary at the same time as I was, and he's the perfect example of a volunteer who is always there for the right reasons. He has a dozen years of volunteering under his belt, and he absolutely loves the game of hockey.

Charles' role on the Board was to manage and administer discipline inside the game of minor hockey in Calgary. In other words, he was the guy who dealt with investigation of any issues that came to the Board, from coaches who said something to an official, to coaches screaming at other coaches, players being mistreated, and anything else that demanded further attention.

Charles would come to each Thursday night hearing equipped with the most comprehensive reports you could imagine. Coming from many years of corporate experience, at the end of which I was the president of a large company, I can say this with confidence: I would have died for reports like that inside the corporate environment! He did an incredible amount of investigative work, and it made the hearings a cinch. We would arrive on Thursday nights, have discussions about the cases, verify and validate some of the information he gave us in his report, and then we would be able to go home to our families, satisfied that we had made the right decisions.

It was a delight to work with Charles. He is an unbelievable individual in the right job, doing work he has the skills and competencies to do very well. If all volunteers came to minor hockey with such focus, determination, and joy, we wouldn't have anything to talk about.

After mentioning Charles, I have to say that, as the former president of Hockey Calgary, countless volunteers give many, many hours to make the sport what it is. I have seen parents, coaches, and officials give of themselves generously in every possible situation. I absolutely don't take that for granted, and I don't think anyone does. But we need to do a better job of making sure that we don't get complacent. The goal in any minor hockey organization is to get as many volunteers in this category as possible.

Volunteer #2: There for the badge of honor

Our second type of volunteer is the person who does everything for a reason. He wants to show everyone his badge of honor, and then, when it comes time to put work in, he conveniently disappears, allowing Volunteer #1 to do all of the hard work.

Let me tell a short story of a man I will call John. He was very pleased to be chosen as a member of Hockey Calgary's Board.

I vividly remember a discussion I had with John at the very beginning, when he was talking about all of the wonderful things he was going to do, and all of the things he wanted to get involved with. We gave John (who seemed to be very excited) a prominent role on the Board based on his skills and competencies, but as the year progressed, we quickly realized that John was not really there.

In the first month, when we were just getting to know John, he seemed just like Ian (Volunteer #1). He spoke with us about how hard he was going to work, and how excited he was about his new role. He said all the right things.

Then, after the first month, John's actions changed our perception of what he really intended to contribute. The grim reality was, John loved to wear the jacket, and he showed up at the annual general meeting, and every function that had a high profile, because he wanted to make sure he got his accolades (as a volunteer on the Board). But John never took on a single assignment. He gave no contribution to any of the extracurricular activity that all Board members are asked to take part in.

At the end of the year, we asked John to leave. All he had been was a warm body in a chair, and the rest of us had to pick up the slack where he didn't pull his weight.

Whether or not "John" is fictional is not important. This type of volunteer is very real – avoid him like the plague. Nothing good will come from his involvement.

Volunteer #3: There for self-serving reasons

The third volunteer is the most damaging type of volunteer. I have many examples of this type of individual in the minor hockey system. He or she comes in many forms, not isolated to gender.

Volunteer #3 is in the system at every level, and is very good at disguising him- or herself, in order to infiltrate the organization. Once they are in, they find ways to get what they want, yet are like chameleons, always changing colours, making sure they don't get caught.

The one and only nice thing about Volunteer #3 is they are only there while their primary purpose in life is in the system, their child – so they won't be around very long. Once their son or daughter has finished hockey, there is no reason for them to stay. Their mission is accomplished. Their mission is/was (only) to look after their child's interest. How do they do this?

Volunteer #3 has only one motive. To advance his/her child's progress in the system, whether that means to a particular team, association, playing time or to the elite structure. When you see and identify this volunteer they will already be embedded in the system and their motives will become clearer and clearer. He/she can be found in any role, but the most prominent roles are those that have an impact on his/her son or daughter. I have found them to be coaches, evaluators, Board members, association presidents, and virtually every volunteer position that could have a direct impact on their child.

You need to call them out! If you are the position of authority (and assume you are not them) you need to ask them to leave. If you are another volunteer or parent and notice their existence, step in!

There is a reoccurring theme here. In order to change our path with all the issues we have in minor hockey, we need to take action. Volunteer #3 is very destructive to the entire system. They are only allowed to exist in this environment because it is a volunteer position and not enough people are prepared to get involved. We need to start embracing the approach of having more people volunteer, and have each of them required to do less. We discussed this earlier – it's so important that the *right* volunteers step up and get involved.

Whenever I have conversations about these types of volunteers, people get it. I would be hard pressed to find anyone who doesn't understand that volunteer-based organizations require dedicated people, all serving the cause and doing what is right to make sure that the best processes, the best scheduling, and the best rules and regulations are followed. We have this selfless group of individuals called volunteers that are serving their community. Everyone gets that. Everyone talks about volunteers, and they understand what needs to be provided in order for volunteer organizations to mobilize themselves and provide greatness to communities.

If Hockey Calgary, Hockey Alberta, and Hockey Canada – on all levels of minor hockey in Canada – didn't have loyal volunteers working hard every week to keep the game afloat, the prices would be prohibitive, and the entire system would collapse on itself. It's a no-brainer that we need great volunteers. The problem is when we have infestations and outbreaks of volunteers who tend to be like Volunteer #2 and Volunteer #3.

What's the solution? First of all, we need to continue to have people in the Volunteer #1 category continue to come out to games, support their local kids, and have a great time in minor hockey. Second of all, when volunteers do step up, they need to be properly evaluated, so that they can be placed into a role where their skills and competencies can best be used and appreciated. These volunteers need to say how much time and energy they will be able to commit to their volunteering, so that they don't turn into Volunteer #2 by design or by mistake.

What the solution should *not* be, in my opinion, is an attitude that volunteerism should go away from the sport. Many parents simply say, "Let me write a cheque, and you can hire a coach, and we don't have to have as many volunteers." The more that attitude exists, and people aren't prepared to go back to the old fashioned basic premise of helping each other and "doing onto others as you want done to yourself," the more we price ourselves out of the ability to have our children participate in the sport. Would you enroll your kid if it cost $3,000 or $4,000 per year?

No, the answer really is that people have to get involved, they got to step up, say, "Here is what I'm able to do, and here's what I have the skills to do." In fact, it doesn't matter if we have 4,500 volunteers in Hockey Calgary or 4,000. If all 4,000 volunteers are like Volunteer #1, quite literally, having more people doing less is the solution, or in this case, fewer people (the *right* people) doing less.

We also need to do a better job of adequately fil-
tering and educating the volunteers, so that their
skills, competencies, and time donations can best
be used to benefit the kids.

Volunteering for minor hockey has been an incredible joy in my life, and I hope I speak for
many of our volunteers when I say that it really
helped me to build my relationship with my son in
his formative years.

When T.J. was in his early days of hockey, he
would say to me, "Dad, why don't you coach?"

In those days, I was very busy with my day job,
and I knew that I wouldn't be able to make that
kind of commitment, so I chose to become the
Team Manager. From my office, I was able to
work on the team list, make sure that people were
informed about practices and game schedules, and
I could organize the tournament events. I was able
to find a job that allowed me to be involved, but
didn't create an undue burden for me. After that I
was able to participate in more capacities, particularly when I was able to slow down the pace of my
life after my company was sold. But even when I
was working a rat-race corporate job, I was still
able to take part.

You can make it that much more enjoyable for both your child and yourself when you get involved for the right reasons, and when you have the right skills, competencies, and time availability; it can be an unbelievable experience. It is not being done for monetary gain; this is just being done because you love your kid, you are a good person, you've got a good heart, and you want to see kids succeed. I also built many incredible, lifelong relationships as a direct result of my getting involved as a volunteer with my son's hockey teams.

As a volunteer, you can't ever put a dollar value to the smiles on these kids' faces, and the satisfaction of seeing a successful season go by. As the president of Hockey Calgary, some of my best moments were at the end of the year, putting medals around young players' necks at the end of the season; seeing these kids and their satisfaction after working so hard throughout the year.

So, after all of this positive messaging around volunteering, I encourage you to go out there, strap on your Moron Helmet, and be a moron. Get out there – your kid needs you. Go climb the glass like Spider-Man, and yell and scream at a twelve-year-old referee. Your kid will thank you for it when they get older. Really.

Please forgive my sarcasm – but this is what is all around the game. Log onto YouTube any day of the week in Canada, and you will see videos that people have captured of adults acting like absolute morons around the game of minor hockey.

At the end of the day, think about your kids. What will they think of Daddy swearing at some other dad, then punching him in the head? Let's never forget this is about the kids. Children are playing the game because it's supposed to be fun, and because it can build their ability, their integrity, and their personality.

Many people call hockey a "religion" in Canada. That's not far from the truth. But we have to remember that the "win" is not the god we should worship inside of that "religion." Instead, we need to help our children have an unbelievable experience. We, as volunteers, can share in their youthful energy and spirit, if we get involved for the right reasons. So, do your own self-assessment about your skills, competencies, and how much time you are able to dedicate. Then get involved!

THE BEHIND THE SCENES STORY OF MINOR HOCKEY

PART FOUR:
THE PLAYERS

Chapter Ten
THE MOST POWERFUL MAN IN HOCKEY

*"You make a living, by what you get.
You make a life by what you give."*

- (attributed to) Winston Churchill

I was sitting in a very large conference room at the Hockey Alberta Annual General Meeting while individuals were voted into various positions. My lot in life is that I was about to be voted in as the new president of the world's largest hockey association, Hockey Calgary.

As I sat at my table, a colleague of mine looked across at me and said, "You're about to become the most powerful man in hockey."

At the time my colleague said those words to me, I thought to myself, "Really? Could this role really be labeled the 'most powerful man in hockey?'

And, if so, is this something that I'm really interested in in being part of?"

Initially, I kind of sloughed off the comment, thinking what he had said was a bit embarrassing, and overly arrogant, and quite frankly, not what I'm all about or what I wanted anything to do with."

Years before, I had been at the top of the world in business, when I was involved in the largest single transactional sale in Bain Capital's history (the sale of my company made Bain a profit of $700 million dollars in the period of less than a year). And, as I describe in my book, *Boardroom to Base Camp*, I made a decision to get out of that world. A fellow businessman told me, "It's never enough." I made a decision that I had enough – and I certainly didn't want to be the "most powerful man" anytime soon again, in any capacity.

The reality is, I was entering a position of great influence that might be interpreted as one of great power as well. I had the ability to influence the game of hockey in many ways, both positive and negative, but what I found most important was not to exercise the power I had been given, but to keep it in check, and remember that this game was all about the 13,500 children of Hockey Calgary, playing a game they loved. It was my job not to be powerful, but to be balanced and humble.

Let's think for a moment about a motion that was put on the floor of a meeting that called for creating a safer environment for children within the game of hockey. At that meeting, the Board agreed to establish a body checking committee, and a dozen volunteers would commit to reviewing all of the facts on the issue, and come back with a report that would influence our decision on how to move forwards.

That committee would prove to teach us a powerful message about influence. As much as we thought we did a careful screening of the individuals that were going to be in that room, we had some bullying going on. We had one individual in the room that was pretty adamant about his particular views, and he was going to try to bully the room into his way of thinking. We had another individual in the room that was pretty adamant on the other side of the fence – with a compassionate, motherly plea against body checking.

We also lacked leadership in the group; the kind of neutral and impartial leadership we required. As a matter of fact, the leader of the group was discovered to be pretty one-sided, as we discovered after the fact.

Problems became more and more evident as the time elapsed, and several times I had to step in and have conversations with the team to try to get them back on track. Again, here was the issue of volunteers signing up for important jobs, yet not stepping up to the plate when the time came, based on skills, competencies, and allocation of time.

There is no easy solution, and there's no easy fix. There is no, "pop this, take two of these pills in the morning, everything's going to be okay," answer. And in minor hockey, which is 99 years old, it's hard to make change.

What is most interesting to me in a volunteer environment versus a for-profit environment, I have found, is that it takes about three times as long to invoke change in the non-profit world of minor hockey. In a corporate environment, I would be confident that I could lay out a change plan, and in three years I could fully execute virtually any plan, from a complete overhaul of any organization, from the mailroom all the way to the executive suite.

In a volunteer environment, that same type of thinking, and that same type of significant change, in terms of hierarchy, governments, modeling and all the changes that we've been talking about in this book, would take you upwards to nine years inside this same environment. It's a long journey.

Even though it will take a lot of momentum and energy, the only real solution is an executive or corporate solution to the problems of minor hockey.

We need to take a very systematic approach of laying out a business plan, laying out exactly what the goals and objectives are, and having a strategic plan around where we want to be inside the next three years. Tackling that with renewed recruitment efforts to having the right people in the right positions.

When I think about a business planning exercise, it really comes down to asking four critical questions. I've attempted to do that for minor hockey in a very cursory way below.

Question 1. What do you do? What services do you provide? What are the offerings?

Question 2. How do you do it? How do you provide the service that you offer? How do you get your message out? How do you market yourself? Do we do it with all volunteers? Do we have some paid staff? Do we need facilities? Do we rent facilities?

Question 3. Who do we do it for? You know, who cares? Who wants our volunteer service? Or who wants our product, in this case, the game of hockey? Again, you have to go through the details of who is it? It's children, and in what age groups? Who are these children? Are they across the city? Are they just in a particular area in the city? You get great demographic profiling from that kind of data.

Question 4. Why do you do it? Why does anybody even care about this particular service that you provide? And inside of that there will be a financial aspect. It's a not-for-profit environment in the context that you're not expected to make money, but you are expected to balance the books.

So ultimately if you're asking yourself those four questions and setting up your business plan for your volunteer environment, in this case, the game of minor hockey, what is it that we do? How do we do it? How do we provide this particular service that we're interested in doing? Who cares? Who wants it? Who wants the service? And the bigger question at the end is: why do we do it?

The problems in minor hockey are growing every year. As I mentioned earlier, scan YouTube, or visit my blog, and you will see countless posts of morons yelling, fighting, and worse.

At this point, problems only make up five percent of the whole – and 95 percent of hockey is problem-free. Many volunteers have told me through the years, "Let's all focus on the positive." While I am an optimist by nature, I believe that in this situation, you need to keep absolute focus on the positive attributes of anything we're involved with, but we still need to make sure not to ignore the three to five percent that we've identified in previous chapters.

I would take this one step further and suggest that, if we don't embrace this type of approach, the problem is going to continue to grow. The numbers of participants in Hockey Canada are going to continue to drop. Whether that will be due to bullying, because of the wrong volunteers doing the wrong jobs, a safety issue, a cost issue, or availability of facilities, we need to acknowledge that trend, and make a move to feed the plant.

A three to five percent problem will then soon become a ten percent problem, and that is ultimately going to lead towards the demise of hockey in Canada as it is today.

Chapter Eleven
THE BULLIES

We usually think of bullies as children on a school playground who bully another child. From my perspective, as it relates to minor hockey and this great game that we love so much, when we really strip it down and go back through this book chapter by chapter, we return to the common thread that the *real* bullies inside the game of minor hockey are not the players, but the adults.

Think about it. Where is the bully problem? Where's the moronic behaviour? Where are all of the issues coming out of the game of hockey? They are not with the children.

Sure, there's a bad situation that occurs from time to time on the ice, where a child hits another child incorrectly, the referee sees it, and then the kid gets a penalty, where they have to sit in the penalty box or be suspended from the game. We watch out for that kind of thing. We also watch out for inappropriate behaviours and bullying in the dressing room, where kids might bully one of their teammates.

However, the regulations that are in place to deal with child bullies are quite strong, and they are also the ones who are the most easily disciplined in terms of the rules, regulations, guidelines, and hierarchy that is in place for hockey. You know, when we really strip down all of the real absolute key issues that we need to fix as a society, far beyond the game of hockey, it's the behaviour of adults that is the problem.

From the Spider-Man father, climbing up the frickin' glass, banging on it and screaming at the top of his lungs at the twelve-year-old official on the ice, or screaming at his child because he did not do a breakout play properly, to the coach standing up on top of the boards screaming at the top of his lungs at the official, or at his players for not behaving properly, shouting, "skate harder" or "hit him," there are many moronic behaviours that we see in and out of the game. But, ultimately, this is a hockey game, and it's all about the kids, and adults need to be more cognizant of the behaviours they are modeling.

We're not talking about a NHL game. We're not watching guys making millions of dollars playing a game. We are watching children in community rinks out there for the sole benefit of achieving some physical fitness, establishing camaraderie with friends, learning rules and regulations, and being in a respectful environment with coaches. That's what we're talking about here, and the people who are spoiling this – the real bullies – are the adults.

The truth is, even when bullying happens among kids, the responsibility for it usually lies in some part with the adults. Unfortunately, the most common form of bullying these days happens as a result of cellphones with cameras. In this age of social media and technology, pictures from the locker room are sometimes sent around.

The reality of the situation is, this should never have happened in the first place, if adults had been following the rules. Inside of the minor hockey rules, as they are laid out today, there must always be two adults in every dressing room in a minor hockey situation in Hockey Canada. That is the rule, but many adults don't know the rule, and coaches aren't enforcing the rule -- many of them ignoring the occurrence of the problem.

If the bullying rules were properly enforced, as written, you would seldom have problems with a child being disrespectful, abusive, or bullying another human being, let along taking a photograph of another boy in the locker room. Second of all, the added protection of having two adults in every locker room situation helps guard against, God forbid, the situation where you end up with an adult who takes advantage of that child's trust.

The other thing is the importance of an education component when it comes to kids. Hockey Canada has embraced a program called Respect in Sport, and they have just launched a new program. Their goal is to educate kids more and more, in terms of what bullying looks like. That will, and has, made all the difference. Only, not with adult bullies. That problem still exists.

Picture, for a moment, some person in your neighborhood saying to you, "You know what? I'm going to start using your sprinkler. I'm going to use your water to water my lawn, and that's the way it's going to be, because I'm the biggest guy on the street."

That situation sounds ridiculous – it just wouldn't happen. And yet, suddenly, in the game of minor hockey, when an adult sees his child being neglected by the coach, is sitting him on the bench and obviously that child knows what happening.

He's not getting played because I guess he's not as good as the other players on the team and I see it, and parents have come to me in the past and said, "It's just horrible. I'm so upset about this," and when I invariably ask them, "So what are you going to do about it?" Parents reply with, "Oh well, I can't do anything about it because then Johnny will no longer be able to play on this elite level team next year."

When we think about that, and anybody that would read those statements, read that story, I would challenge you to say, 'Is that acceptable?' Is that remotely, in any concept, is that an acceptable behaviour by an adult to not step up to defend their child, for fear of retribution from the coach?

What is even worse is what are we teaching the child at the center of this mess. What are we teaching your child as you jump in the car or truck that night, and as you drive home from the rink, Little Johnny says, "Boy, Dad, I don't get to play very much; the coach doesn't play me. He must not like me, or I'm not the strongest of players, so I guess I shouldn't be playing hockey." That's just not the way things should operate.

The solution needs to come from the bottom up; from the majority of adults who are *not* the bullies; from the majority who are *not* morons.

The majority of adults inside this game are really, really good, decent people and that's where the solution comes from. It comes from them showing a sincere and active interest in getting involved, speaking out, and not putting up with bullying behaviour when they witness it.

Instead of sitting back and waiting for the system to deal with the adult's inappropriate bullying behaviour, or the inappropriate behaviour in a volunteer rank, or the inappropriate behaviour as a coach, parents need to speak up and not allow themselves to be bullied. The vast majority of parents are great people and they want nothing but greatness to occur inside this game. So the solution comes from not sitting back waiting for the hierarchy or the system to fix it. The system has all the right rules and regulations in place. It's time to fix the problem of systemic adult bullying from the bottom up.

The problem is parents or adults are not prepared to step up for fear of retribution, for fear of isolation, for fear of legacy issues as a result of them stepping up and saying 'look this is just unacceptable'. The more and more people that step up to that, against the bullies, against the adults that are misbehaving, the quicker we can fix the problem. But it will take action from good people to prevail over these bullies.

Chapter Twelve
MORON HELMET

In the first chapter of this book, I introduced the concept of the Moron Helmet. I'd like to go back to that in a moment, but first I'd like to talk about where that idea came from.

Search in your favorite search engine for "magic helmet" and you will see the three-minute YouTube video that's been shared all over the place. It's a video of a nine-year-old boy who passionately and articulately shares his views about what is really going on when kids are on the ice.

When this young boy puts on his helmet to start the hockey game, he calls it a magic helmet – because all of the adults suddenly treat him like a grownup. When he's on the ice, playing minor hockey, after he puts his magic helmet on, he is disrespected, yelled at, and can seemingly do nothing right. The boy thinks, "When I'm on the ice, playing minor hockey after I put on my magic helmet, they clearly start treating me with disrespect and yelling and screaming at me. So clearly this helmet must be magical because those people would otherwise never treat a nine-year-old boy like they treat me once I put this helmet on."

If that nine-year-old is putting on a Magic Helmet, the adults around him all too often put on their Moron Helmet. And, all of a sudden, a normal dad is climbing up the boards like Spider-Man.

To be honest, I've had the Moron Helmet on myself a time or two. Hockey can be a very passionate game, and we can get very emotionally connected to the outcome of our children's games. I remember being in situations where the score is tied, and we're in the last seconds, and all of a sudden, the official makes a call that I don't think is a good one, so I say out loud, "Ahh! How could you make that call? It's ridiculous!" Yeah, I know, I had my Moron Helmet on. But not for long.

So where does this moronic behaviour come from? It's not present in other minor sports as much, or at all. The answer is, part of the reason minor hockey ends up having so much moronic behaviour from parents, spectators, coaches, and others, is that hockey behaviour is learned from spectating professional games.

Fans enter hockey arenas to be part of the crowd, booing, hissing, clapping, cheering, and eating, and to be drawn into the drama of the game. The hockey stars are paid professionals, and people attend the game to be entertained, not just to see who wins. Some of the tickets even sell for hundreds of dollars. It's not uncommon to hear of a family going off to a hockey and dropping five hundred dollars on a hockey game, if not more. That again is how passionate people are about the game.

So when they are there, they expect to be entertained. They expect to enjoy the event. They expect to get fully engaged, cheering for fights and injuries as well as goals scored and plays made. They scream at the referees, and they jeer the other team. The kind of behaviour that is acceptable at a major ice arena is not acceptable rink side at a kids' hockey game.

The moron helmet has to be left in the truck, or in the car. It can't come into that arena. And when you arrive there, you actually have to take on a leadership role. You are an adult – a role model for these kids. Instead of acting moronically, you have the opportunity to actually become somebody that's so observant to moronic behaviour that you're going to start to invoke change.

When Spider-Man is climbing up the glass, you will be the one to tug his pant leg and ask him to step down. All adults who are associated with minor hockey have to get engaged and solve the problem.

People need to step up and become more involved. That is the real solution to this problem, yet again. The top down approach, where Hockey Canada works with the branches, and the branches work with the local associations, and the local associations work with coaches, and the kids and players will work with the coach and the parents — won't work. Parents have a much larger role than simply paying the registration fees and then putting their kids into the hands of others. In fact, they have the most important role.

Once a parent makes the choice to put their child into minor hockey, their job is to educate their child as well as they can. They also need to make a committed effort to become educated as to their role as a parent. It's not as easy as it might seem on the surface! Materials for both of these are available through Hockey Canada online.

What this ultimately comes down to is that playing hockey as a part of Hockey Canada is not a must. It's a membership. It's a privilege. It's not an obligation. It's a choice that you make, and once you make the choice as a parent, you should get your child involved, so they can understand exactly what the commitment is that you are making. There is an expense commitment. There is a time commitment. There is a volunteer commitment. There is a commitment to educate your child, in order to make sure they understand what they are doing. There is a commitment to make sure you're a proper custodian of the environment which you're in. In other words, you commit to be a defender against bullies, and someone who can help curb moronic behaviour in others (and yourself).

If we are able to start from the bottom, we will not only transform the behaviour of adults surrounding the game, we will also transform the child. If the child sees great behaviour coming from the parent, they will model that behaviour.

This will foster a community of adults that is not afraid to call someone out when they violate the Fair Play rules, or when they do something moronic. They will not be afraid to replace a coach who is inappropriately leaving children alone in a dressing room.

At the end of the day, we are talking about adults embracing a leadership role as it relates to the game of hockey. Being a leader is part of being a parent, and this is the logical extension of that role.

I will assume that the vast majority of people are very good people, so in that context we have a leadership role here to care for others, to treat others like we want to be treated, to make sure that we keep our Moron Helmet off our own head, and whenever we see somebody who maybe slips up, we step in as leaders and advise that person something like, "Hey, you know, that's really not the most appropriate behaviour," or, "That really wasn't very Respect-in-Sport-like."

The point is, we are the adults. We are the real leaders of this minor hockey organization. You shouldn't be relying on the President or the Board of Directors, in isolation, to step up and take a stand. They are not the most powerful people in hockey. You are.

I love the game of hockey. Heck, I am a Canadian. I have played the game, and I coached kids to play the game. I still get out there and referee every season.

That's where I'm coming from. Because I love the game so much, I see that if we don't start to change things from the bottom up, I see the game eroding. But I see the path forward, and I see steps being made – and we have the ability to shape the future of minor hockey in Canada.

At the end of the day, it's about our kids. We want the best for them. We want them to be safe, but also to be exposed to new experiences, and incredible challenges. From the ages of five to 18, we want our kids to hear the cheer of the crowd, feel the thrill of a goal, experience the disappointment of a tough loss. We want them to become great skaters, good puck handlers, and ultimately, good people.

That's all this is about; allowing children to play this unbelievable game, having unbelievable experiences that they'll cherish for the rest of their life just as we had as children. My dad was in the stands cheering for me, and I was in the stands cheering for my son. My hope is that he'll be there in a decade or more, cheering for his own son. There is a great future ahead for minor hockey in Canada if we make a concerted effort today.

Let's work hard to make the concepts of the Magic Helmet and the Moron Helmet irrelevant in a discussion about minor hockey. Children should play, adults should lead, and there should be only one objective in mind: respect. Let's bring this game back to its basics: an unbelievable game with a stick and puck on ice.

About the Author

Todd Millar was formally involved with one of the most successful Private Equity transactions in the history of Bain Capital – the acquisition of SuperPages Canada for $1.9 billion dollars, and less than a year later, its sale for $2.6 billion dollars. After 25 years in senior executive positions in the petroleum, telecommunications, and advertising industries, Millar is now a national speaker and executive coach, as well as immediate Past-President of the world's largest hockey association, Hockey Calgary. He has been involved in a number of volunteer organizations, including various hockey organizations, the Juvenile Diabetes Research Foundation, the Calgary Stampede and the National Adoption Association.

If you can't find Millar on the ice officiating a hockey game, he might be scuba diving, climbing to Base Camp of Everest or zip lining across a rain forest.

Find out more at *www.toddmillarspeaking.com*

Acknowledgments

Thank you to: the Hockey Calgary Board of Directors; Kirk Reynolds, Past-GM of Hockey Calgary; the Hockey Calgary staff; countless volunteers in "Group #1"; Hockey Canada (specifically Bob Nicholson and Paul Carson for their leadership); the hockey branches across Canada, specifically: Hockey Alberta, Central Zone Executive, and the officials of CZRC; Dr. Carolyn Emery and her team; all of the great professionals calling attention to safety aspects in the game for the benefit of the children; Provoke and Trudy White-Matthews; Wayne McNeil and Sheldon Kennedy, for their work with Respect in Sport; Safer Hockey Canada (especially Andrea Winarski and all of her supporters, for their commitment and dedication); all of the parents who support their children in minor hockey; most importantly, the children who just want to play the game.

Useful Resources

WEBSITES
http://www.thinkfirst.ca
http://www.stopconcussions.com
http://www.playitcoolhockey.com
http://www.biac-aclc.ca
http://www.cdc.gov/concussion
http://www.sportslegacy.org
http://www.momsteam.com

MORE RESOURCES
Please visit www.toddmillarspeaking.com/hockey for more
resources, and www.toddmillarspeaking.com/blog for news
and updates about the body checking debate and much more.

CPSIA information can be obtained at www.ICGtesting.com
Printed in the USA
LVOW121822010513

331850LV00002B/2/P